THE LITTLE BOOK OF BIG MANAGEMENT THEORIES

James McGrath
Bob Bates

THE LITTLE BOOK OF BIG MANAGEMENT THEORIES

... AND HOW TO USE THEM

PEARSON

Harlow, England • London • New York • Boston • San Francisco • Toronto • Sydney
Auckland • Singapore • Hong Kong • Tokyo • Seoul • Taipei • New Delhi
Cape Town • São Paulo • Mexico City • Madrid • Amsterdam • Munich • Paris • Milan

PEARSON EDUCATION LIMITED

Edinburgh Gate
Harlow CM20 2JE
United Kingdom
Tel: +44 (0)1279 623623
Web: www.pearson.com/uk

First edition published 2013 (print and electronic)

ISBN: 978-0-273-78526-2 (print)
      978-0-273-78878-2 (PDF)
      978-0-273-78877-5 (ePub)
      978-1-292-00831-8 (eText)

British Library Cataloguing-in-Publication Data
A catalogue record for the print edition is available from the British Library

Library of Congress Cataloging-in-Publication Data
McGrath, James, 1952-
   The little book of big management theories ... and how to use them / James McGrath, Bob Bates. -- First edition.
      pages cm
   ISBN 978-0-273-78526-2 (pbk.) -- ISBN 978-0-273-78878-2 (PDF) -- ISBN 978-0-273-78877-5 (ePub) -- ISBN 978-1-292-00831-8 (eText)
   1. Management. 2. Employee motivation. 3. Organizational change. I. Bates, Bob, 1951- II. Title.
   HD31.M3834 2013
   658.3--dc23
                        2013032076

10 9 8 7
17 16 15

Text design by Design Deluxe
Cover design by Nick Redeyoff
Print edition typeset in Helvetica Neue LT Pro 9.5pt by 3
Print edition printed and bound in Great Britain by Ashford Colour Press Ltd.

NOTE THAT ANY PAGE CROSS REFERENCES REFER TO THE PRINT EDITION

For Eija, Michael, Helen, Patrick and little Finbar – welcome to the world.
Also in memory of Andrew Soares (1980–2011).

For Val and the grandkids.

CONTENTS

About the authors xi
Acknowledgements xii
Introduction xiii
How to get the most out of this book xvi

SECTION 1 HOW TO MANAGE PEOPLE 1

Introduction 3
1   Fayol's 14 principles of management: Part 1 – structure and control 4
2   Fayol's 14 principles of management: Part 2 – working relationships 6
3   Taylor and scientific management 8
4   Mayo and the Hawthorne experiments 10
5   Urwick's ten principles of management 12
6   Drucker on the functions of management 14
7   McGregor's X and Y theory 16
8   Peters and Waterman's theory of management 18
9   Covey's seven habits™ of highly effective people 20
10 Management by walking about (MBWA) 22
A final word on management theories 24

SECTION 2 HOW TO LEAD PEOPLE 27

Introduction 28
11 Trait theory 30
12 The Michigan and Ohio studies – basic style theory 32
13 Blake and Mouton's leadership grid® 34
14 Adair's action-centred leadership 36
15 Fiedler's contingency theory 38
16 Hersey and Blanchard's situational leadership theory 40
17 Burns' transactional leadership theory 42
18 Dansereau, Graen and Haga's leader member exchange (LMX) theory 44
19 House's charismatic leadership theory 46
20 Burns' transformational leadership (TL) theory 48
21 Bass and transformational leadership (TL) theory 50

22 Bennis and Nanus' transformational leadership (TL) theory 52
A final word on leadership theories 54

SECTION 3 HOW TO MOTIVATE YOUR STAFF 57

Introduction 58
23 Maslow's hierarchy of needs theory 60
24 Alderfer's existence, relatedness and growth (ERG) theory 62
25 McClelland's achievement and acquired needs theory 64
26 Herzberg's motivation and hygiene theory 66
27 Adams' equity theory 68
28 Vroom's expectancy theory 70
29 The Hackman and Oldham job characteristic model 72
30 Ernst's OK Corral model 74
31 Berne's theory of transactional analysis 76
A final word on motivation theories 78

SECTION 4 HOW TO BUILD AND MANAGE TEAMS 81

Introduction 83
32 Belbin's team roles 84
33 Maccoby's gamesman theory 86
34 Likert's theory of team management styles 88
35 Drexler/Sibbet Team Performance Model® 90
36 Homan's theory of group formation 92
37 Tuckman's group development sequence model 94
38 Wheelan's integrated model of group development 96
39 Locke's goal setting theory 98
A final word on team theories 100

SECTION 5 HOW TO ANALYSE ORGANISATIONAL CULTURE 103

Introduction 104
40 Handy's model of organisational culture 106
41 Deal and Kennedy's risk and feedback model 108
42 Morgan's organisational metaphors 110
43 Graves' cultural leadership theory 112
44 Schein's three levels of organisational culture 114
45 Johnson and Scholes' cultural web 116

46   Hofstede's six cross-organisational dimensions 118
47   Hargreaves and Balkanised cultures 120
      A final word on organisational culture theories 122

SECTION 6 HOW TO MANAGE CHANGE 125

      Introduction 127
48   Kübler-Ross's change cycle 128
49   Shewhart's plan–do–check–act (PDCA) model 130
50   Lewin's unfreeze–change–refreeze model 132
51   Lewin's force field analysis 134
52   Kotter's eight-step approach to change 136
53   Moss Kanter and change masters 138
54   Burke-Litwin's drivers for change 140
55   Egan's shadow-side theory 142
      A final word on change management theories 144

SECTION 7 STRATEGIC MANAGEMENT 147

      Introduction 148
56   Johnson and Scholes' seven stages of strategic planning 150
57   Ansoff's modernist approach to strategic management 152
58   Peters and Waterman's post-modernist approach to strategic
      management 154
59   Quinn, Hamel and Prahalad: the new modernist approach 156
60   The Boston Consulting Group matrix model 158
61   The McKinsey 7-S framework model 160
62   Johnson, Scholes and Wittingham's stakeholder mapping theory 162
63   Porter's value chain theory 164
64   Porter's five forces theory 166
65   SWOT analysis 168
66   PEST/PESTLE analysis 170
67   Scenario planning 172
      A final word on strategic management theories 174

SECTION 8 HOW TO MANAGE QUALITY 177

      Introduction 179
68   Deming's seven deadly diseases 180
69   Juran's quality trilogy 182

70 Crosby's maturity grid 184
71 Peters, Waterman and Austin's excellence model 186
72 Ishikawa's fishbone model 188
73 Imai's Kaizen 5S housekeeping theory 190
74 The benchmarking matrix 192
75 The excellence model 194
   A final word on quality management theories 196

SECTION 9 HOW TO EXERCISE AUTHORITY, POWER AND INFLUENCE 199

   Introduction 200
76 Weber's tripartite classification of authority 202
77 French and Raven's sources of power theory 204
78 Sources of influence 206
79 Machiavelli's guide to survival 210
80 Ronson's psychopath test 212
   A final word on authority, power and influence theories 214

SECTION 10 THE BEST OF THE REST – A MISCELLANY OF GREAT IDEAS FOR MANAGERS 217

   Introduction 219
81 The Pareto principle 220
82 The Eisenhower principle 222
83 Thomas and Kilmann's conflict resolution model 224
84 Grinder and Bandler's Neuro Linguistic Programming (NLP) filtering theory 226
85 Goleman's theory of emotional intelligence 228
86 Boyd's OODA loop 230
87 Luft and Ingram's Johari windows 232
88 SMART goals 234
89 The McNamara fallacy 236
   A final word on the best of the rest 238

   The one theory that shall rule them all, and why we picked it 241
   A very final word 243
   Further reading 245
   Index 246

ABOUT THE AUTHORS

Dr James McGrath qualified as an accountant over 30 years ago and has worked in industry, local government, management consultancy and higher education as an accountant, financial controller, senior manager and course director. He is the co-author of three previous books with Anthony Coles: *Your Education Research Project Companion, Your Teacher Training Handbook* and *Your Education Leadership Handbook*. In 2012 he took early retirement to become a full time writer. He is currently working on a follow up to *The Little Book of Big Management Theories* and is looking forward to spending more time watching his beloved West Bromwich Albion home and away. James is a Fellow of both The Association of Chartered Certified Accountants and the Higher Education Academy and has a BA (Hons.) in Politics, an MA in Education and an Ed.D from the University of Birmingham.

Dr Bob Bates was a Senior Executive in the Civil Service for nearly 20 years and in 1994 he launched the Arundel Group, a management development and training company. He now combines writing with working as a Chief Executive for a charity that promotes education and health in a village in The Gambia. He has a degree in computer studies, Masters degrees in Education and Management and a PhD in Management in the Health Sector. He is also an NLP Master Practitioner and a Fellow of the Institute for Learning.

ACKNOWLEDGEMENTS

We would like to thank all at Pearson Education for their encouragement, enthusiasm and great good humour throughout the writing of this book, especially Rachael Stock, Elie Williams and Eloise Cook. We would also like to thank Chris Bates for the work he did on the figures and Helen McGrath for her comments on the manuscript.

PUBLISHER'S ACKNOWLEDGEMENTS

We are grateful to the following for permission to reproduce copyright material:

Team roles and descriptions in the figure used in Theory 32 courtesy of Belbin Associates; Theory 35 figure is the 12.3 TPModel © 1990–2011 Alan Drexler and David Sibbet; Theory 41 figure adapted from Deal, T. E. and Kennedy, A. A., *Corporate Cultures: Rites and Rituals of Corporate Life* (Penguin, 1988), courtesy of Peters, Fraser & Dunlop; figure in Theory 45 adapted from Johnson, G., Whittington, R. and Scholes, K., *Exploring Strategy: Text and Cases* (9th edn) (Pearson Education, 2011); figure in Theory 60 adapted from The BCG Portfolio Matrix from the Product Portfolio Matrix © 1970, the Boston Consulting Group; figure in Theory 70 adapted from Crosby, P. B., *Quality is Free: The Art of Making Quality Certain* (McGraw-Hill, 1978); figure in Theory 72 adapted from Ishikawa, K., *Guide to Quality Control* (Asian Productivity Organisation, 1986); figure in Theory 75 adapted from the European Foundation for Quality Management, copyright © EFQM 2012 Excellence Model, Brussels, Belgium, www.efqm.org; figure in Theory 83 adapted from 'Conflict and Conflict Management' by Kenneth Thomas in *Handbook of Industrial and Organizational Psychology*, edited by Marvin D. Dunnette, p. 900, 1976. Adapted with permission; figure in Theory 86 adapted from Clayton, M., *Management Models Pocket Book* (Management Pocketbooks, 2009).

In some instances we have been unable to trace the owners of copyright material, and we would appreciate any information that would enable us to do so.

INTRODUCTION

Over the last 100 years thousands of managers, academics and researchers have tried to define what makes a great manager and identify the secrets of effective management. The result is hundreds of management theories, many of which are contradictory. The sheer number of theories makes it difficult for hard-pressed managers to separate great theories from passing fads. Unfortunately, even when a manager does find a great theory it is unlikely that it will come with any advice on how to use it in the workplace. Welcome to the theory practice gap – where managers are armed with the principles of good management but struggle to apply them. This book has been conceived and written to bridge this gap and help:

- the many real-world managers or would-be managers who didn't have the opportunity to do an MBA, are time starved, and simply want to know what the best and most important theories are and how to use them;
- those who have studied management science, and may be familiar with many of the theories, but are struggling to apply them in their business.

The book is short and punchy and has been ruthlessly stripped of all extraneous material. What's left is a description of 89 key management theories that every manager should know. Each theory is summarised and advice given on how to apply it in practice in a series of two-page spreads. This means that it will only take you five minutes to read, understand and be ready to use a theory. Not tomorrow or next week but now, today. All you need to do is give it a try. And if you're worried about making a mistake remember:

> **THE MANAGERS' MOTTO** Failure is the price managers pay for future success. The only failure you can be criticised for is not trying.

Only theories that have repeatedly proved their value in the real world of work have been included in the book (even a couple of our own theories didn't make the final cut). Read, understand, reflect upon and use these theories and you'll be able to hold your own in management discussions with just about anyone.

SEVEN THINGS THIS BOOK WILL DO FOR YOU

The Little Book of Big Management Theories will:

- make you a better manager;
- help you motivate your staff and increase your influence over colleagues;
- increase your ability to get things done;
- get you out of a mental rut and provide you with the confidence to embrace new ideas, visions and ambitions;
- provide you with the key skills you need to demonstrate you are ready for promotion;
- increase your personal capital and earning power; and
- help you identify and understand your management style.

HOW THE BOOK IS ORGANISED

The book is divided into ten sections. The first nine deal with specific areas of management such as motivation or team building. The final section contains a miscellany of great theories, each of which could have been squeezed into one of the other sections. But we kept them separate because they are the all-rounders and can be used in many different situations. For example, the Pareto Principle is as useful when dealing with staff problems as it is in identifying who your important customers are.

Across all ten sections you'll notice that there are two distinct types of theory discussed. In total about 20% deal with the realities of the environment in which you operate. Misread this and you'll find yourself in constant war with the organisation and achieve nothing. The other 80% are about improving your effectiveness as a manager. Get this right and your credibility will soar.

Each entry starts with a box telling you when/where you could use the theory. Obviously this is just a guide and we're sure you'll be able to see other uses. The entry ends with questions you should ask yourself. Many of the same questions apply to several entries but we've tried to avoid repetition. That doesn't mean that you can't repeat the same questions. So, after you've read an entry consider what other questions you could ask.

Naturally there are links and overlaps between the theories. To help you make these connections we've numbered each theory and use that as the linking reference. For example (*see Theory 11*) will send you to the entry on trait theory; whereas (*see Section 3*) will redirect you to Section 3 How to motivate staff.

Within each section one theory is crowned as king/queen of that section and at the end of the book one of the section winners is named as the emperor/empress of all management theories. Let us know what you think of our choices.

AND FINALLY ...

There is a whole literature written by academics and management gurus about the difference between managers and leaders. They suggest that they possess different characteristics and are psychologically very different people. The truth is that anyone who holds a management role has to combine the roles of administrator, manager and leader if they are to do their job effectively. For that reason the term manager is used throughout the book except where specific leadership theories are discussed.

Good luck with your career and we hope you enjoy the book.

James McGrath and Bob Bates
July 2013

HOW TO GET THE MOST OUT OF THIS BOOK

By their nature all management theories are a partial explanation and simplification of the complex reality they try to explain. To expect one theory to fully explain what's going on or to work in all situations is on a par with expecting that a road map of London will help you navigate your way across Europe.

Without a range of management theories and ideas to inform your actions you'll be like the carpenter who only has a hammer in his or her toolbox, with the result that every problem s/he encounters looks like a nail (which sounds like the guy who built my kitchen).

The key phrase in the above paragraph is 'inform your actions'. Some theories will immediately appeal to you. Others you'll reject out of hand. That's fine. Some approaches won't suit your personality and unless they reflect your beliefs about how people should be treated you will find it difficult to use them effectively. What you should do is take from each theory that which is useful to you. But how do you do that? Let's digress for a moment.

Jazz players start off by learning individual tunes. They become expert at playing each tune and if you were in the audience listening you'd be impressed by their skill. That's what you can do with an individual theory. Read the entry and think about: How can I use this theory? In what circumstances can I use it? When will I use it? For example, you might read situational leadership (see Theory 16) and immediately recognise how easy it is to use in practice. You decide to try it the next time you delegate a new job to a member of staff. Three days later an opportunity arises and you try out the new approach. You monitor how successful your approach has been and based on that decide if you are going to use it again, use it with some amendments or abandon it because it didn't suit your personality or fit in with 'how things are done around here' (see Section 5). There is nothing wrong with using each theory in this way. This approach will make you a very competent manager. But you'll never be a jazz legend because you've only learnt the individual tunes.

If you want to be a jazz great you have to learn to improvise. To use the basic tune as a starting point and then let your entire musical knowledge take you on a journey of discovery. The same applies to management. Management is about people. People aren't logical. They aren't machines. You can't apply the same theory with everyone and expect the same result. Here's what you need to do:

- Study the insights (theories) that management theorists have developed over the years.

- Understand how to apply each theory in practice and think about its limitations in terms of what is acceptable in your organisation and your own preferences.

- Observe other managers at work.

- Get to know your staff and what makes them tick.

- Practise your management skills at every opportunity and try out either entire theories or parts of theories discussed in this book.

- Keep a diary, or use the spare space in this book, and record, *very briefly*, your experiences of management: e.g. What happened? Why did it happen? What could I have done differently? Why was I successful in that situation but failed in another? Learn from these mini reflections and use them to guide your future actions.

Writing a few reflective notes will help you internalise what you have learnt. As your knowledge is broken down into its constituent parts it will be added to the compost bin that resides in the dark recesses of your unconscious. It is there where it will mingle with your own emotions, beliefs and attitudes to form your own bank of tacit knowledge. When required, this unconscious knowledge will inform every management action and decision you make and from that will flow your own unique management style and soon you'll be improvising with the masters.

Don't believe me? You think that all this talk of tacit knowledge and reflection is a load of management guru bull****? OK. When was the last time you were in a meeting and your boss said, 'We're going to do X from next month' and immediately you knew it was a bad idea. Doomed to crash and burn ignominiously but you couldn't explain why? That's your tacit knowledge at work. A previous generation called it gut instinct. It's so real that Friedrich von Hayek, Nobel Laureate for Economics, used it as one of the pillars to support his free market theories. It was his ideas that changed the face of British and American economic policy in the 1980s and which remains with us to this day.

SECTION 1

HOW TO MANAGE PEOPLE

INTRODUCTION

n this section you'll find two types of theories. The first comes from the very early days of management when writers tried to identify and describe the functions of management. They tell you what you should be doing. The second type tells you how you should do it.

The one thing that none of the theories say is 'To thine own self be true' (Shakespeare, *Hamlet*). What this means in management terms is that if you try to copy someone else's approach you will fail. You have to become the unique manager that you were meant to be. That doesn't mean that you can't have role models.

By all means copy the actions of managers you admire. Read the biographies of managers that make the best-seller list. But remember you are not them. You don't share their personality, life experiences, training or skills. Nor do you currently run a multi-billion pound organisation or have the power that they enjoy. Successful entrepreneurs have the power and influence to be as colourful and maverick as they want. If you act like them before you've made it you'll probably be regarded as one of those workplace psychopaths that we discuss in Theory 80 and be invited to leave.

Instead, take what you read and adopt and adapt those ideas, or parts of ideas, that appeal to you. Those you feel comfortable with and which you think will work in your organisation. Don't use any approach that you feel uncomfortable with.

Having observed managers in action, done a bit of reading on management theory, looked at other successful managers and gained hands-on experience of managing, your own unique management style will evolve. Continue to feed its development through reading, observation, thinking and analysis.

The more you know about your management style and how it impacts upon other people the more effective you'll be. But remember, it's always easier to con your boss into believing that you're a great manager than your own staff. Like your partner, staff see the real you day-in and day-out. So seek feedback from them and address any weaknesses they identify.

THEORY 1 FAYOL'S 14 PRINCIPLES OF MANAGEMENT: PART 1 – STRUCTURE AND CONTROL

Use to remind you that as a manager you must use your authority to ensure that the organisation's structure and systems for managing staff and resources are working effectively.

Henri Fayol's 14 principles of management first appeared in *Administration industrielle et generale* (1916). The relationships between employers, managers and staff have changed since then, as has the terminology used. However, Fayol's insights remain relevant.

Fayol believed that managers had a responsibility to ensure that the organisation's structure was effective and fit for purpose and that they must manage human and other resources effectively.

HE BELIEVED THAT MANAGERS SHOULD:
Exercise authority.
Ensure that unity of command exists.
Ensure that there is a clear chain of command within the organisation.
Provide unity of direction for all staff.
Manage the supply of human and other resources.
Exercise staff discipline.
Coordinate key activities through centralisation.

HOW TO USE IT

- You have the right to direct staff and expect compliance. If you fail to use your authority *(see Theories 76 and 77)* staff will think you weak. Don't be embarrassed, shy or doubtful when giving instructions *(see Theory 11)*. If someone fails to comply with your request don't ignore it. Repeat your request and if they continue to ignore you look at what sanctions you can apply *(see Theory 17)*. Under no circumstances capitulate and do the job yourself.

- Promote what Fayol called unity of direction, i.e. in any organisation there can only be one head, one plan and one vision. Ensure that staff understand the chain of command (authority), are familiar with the organisation's structure and where they fit into it and that they are committed to the organisation's aims.

- Organise your team on the basis that everyone reports to a single line manager. If someone has two managers disputes over work priorities will arise and your staff will play one manager off against another.

- You want a relationship with staff that is based on mutual respect, trust and frankness. However, this does not mean that discipline should be sacrificed. There will be rules of behaviour in your organisation, many of them unwritten, which you must apply consistently to all staff including yourself.

- You are responsible for ensuring that staff have the right resources at the right time to do their job. Staff will judge you on how successful you are at obtaining these resources. Constantly monitor the situation, predict future requirements and move to fill any shortfalls immediately. Think ahead.

- Always place the needs of the organisation above your own or those of your team. If the organisation fails then you and all your staff are out of a job. So avoid sub-optimisation even if it makes you or your team look good.

QUESTIONS TO ASK

- Do any of my team report to two or more managers?
- Are my team's aims and objectives aligned with those of the organisation?

THEORY 2 FAYOL'S 14 PRINCIPLES OF MANAGEMENT: PART 2 – WORKING RELATIONSHIPS

Use when you need to quickly review your key responsibilities to the organisation and staff.

Given that Henri Fayol started work as an engineer in 1860, he held surprisingly modern views concerning the treatment of staff by the organisation.

FAYOL ARGUED THAT MANAGERS SHOULD:
Seek efficiency through the division of work.
Subordinate their needs and those of their team to the needs of the organisation.
Ensure that staff are fairly remunerated.
Ensure equity of treatment for all staff.
Provide job security as far as possible.
Encourage staff initiative.
Establish a sense of *esprit de corps* (team spirit).

HOW TO USE IT

- The division of work into a series of repetitive tasks is no longer acceptable. Today people expect fulfilment from their job *(see Section 3)*. However, more effective and efficient ways of working can nearly always be found. Review annually the allocation of work and working practices within your team.

- You must subordinate your needs and those of your team to those of the organisation. In the long run you will benefit as you will be seen as someone who sees the bigger picture.

- Your pay and that of your staff should be comparable with others in the organisation doing a similar job. Wide differentials cause resentment and undermine teamwork *(see Theory 27)*. Monitor pay rates and take action when required.

- Staff want consistency and fairness from their manager. If you are inconsistent in your actions you will create uncertainty in the minds of staff. By all means be friendly and approachable but remember that one day you may have to discipline or sack one of your team so maintain a professional distance.

- You cannot afford to have favourites. You must treat all staff equitably.

- New staff will become proficient quicker if you make them feel welcome and secure in their job. Suspend judgement on their performance until they have had sufficient time to show their true worth.

- Encourage all staff to exercise their initiative within clearly defined limits.

- There are many ways to forge team spirit. In the military, *esprit de corps* is built on shared hardship. You might decide that a regular meal out with staff is preferable to a march across the Brecon Beacons in February. Although there will always be one or two people you'd like to send there.

QUESTIONS TO ASK

- Do I have any favourites among the staff?
- Is there any member of staff I dislike dealing with? Do I treat them differently to other staff or over compensate because of my feelings towards them?

THEORY 3 **TAYLOR AND SCIENTIFIC MANAGEMENT**

Use when staff resources are tight and you need to increase productivity.

Frederick Taylor rose from shop floor labourer to become a Director at Bethlehem Steel, the largest steel maker in the United States. He was a contemporary of Fayol but was more interested in efficiency than the social aspects of managing people. His book *The Principles of Scientific Management* (1913) cemented his reputation as the father of scientific management.

TAYLOR:
Believed that the job of a manager was to plan and control work and that there was a single most efficient way to do any job.
Used time and motion techniques to break down each work process into its constituent parts and eliminate unnecessary actions. Using these principles he reduced the number of actions a bricklayer took from 18 to 5 and in the process saved time and money. His work laid the foundation for the division of labour and mass production which Henry Ford applied so successfully in car manufacturing.
Argued that the best way to ensure maximum efficiency was to carefully select and train staff and provide additional opportunities for those that showed potential. This was revolutionary at a time when most workers were given no formal training. Outstanding workers were identified by placing a chalk mark on their work bench *(Benchmarking see Theory 74).*

HOW TO USE IT

- Review how each job is done in your team and ask the following questions: Do we need to do this job? Can it be done more efficiently? Does the work allocated to each member of staff match their abilities/strengths? Do staff need additional training to improve their efficiency and effectiveness.

- Decide how work can be reallocated and reorganised to improve efficiency, increase throughput and play to the individual strengths of staff *(See Section 6).*

- Following reorganisation evaluate how effective the changes have been and tweak as required. It's very unlikely that you will get it right first time.

- Regularly review (at least annually) the work that staff do and look for efficiency gains. If you think that a report you issue is no longer used don't ask the recipients if they need it. They'll almost certainly say 'yes'. Instead, produce the report but don't send it out and see if anyone shouts. If after three months no one has screamed, ditch it.

- Additional training can improve your team's productivity greatly. For example, how sure are you that every member of the team can use all of the facilities available on your computer systems?

- Remember Taylor's ideas don't just apply to the shop floor. Inefficient working practices are rife in most offices.

- When undertaking the review of work canvass ideas from the wider team on how the task could be done more efficiently.

QUESTIONS TO ASK

- Does the team struggle to meet deadlines and/or have periods when they have very little work? If yes, can the timetabling of work be improved?

THEORY 4 **MAYO AND THE HAWTHORNE EXPERIMENTS**

Use in conjunction with Theory 26 to identify the factors that actually motivate staff.

In the late 1920s, Elton Mayo and his team from Massachusetts Institute of Technology carried out a series of experiments with manual workers at General Electric's Hawthorne Plant. The results seemed to defy the received wisdom of the time and continue to be of interest today.

THE HAWTHORNE RESEARCHERS FOUND THAT:

There was no correlation between productivity and working conditions. Productivity went neither up nor down significantly when conditions were either degraded or improved.

Belonging to a group was the single most important motivational factor. Staff found status and a sense of belonging within the group. They feared being excluded from the group or letting their mates down with shoddy work and did everything they could to be seen as a 'good un'. Often these groups were informal in nature and yet they exercised enormous influence over the behaviour of members.

Productivity increased as a result of the researchers and management talking to the staff, asking for their views and treating them as individuals and not just hired hands. Effectively, treating staff with respect and as intelligent individuals paid dividends.

HOW TO USE IT

■ Recognise that working conditions by themselves have very little effect on motivation or productivity. Only when they fall below an acceptable level do they demotivate staff *(see Theory 26)*.

■ Knowing that staff are more motivated when they belong to a group is a key piece of information. Yes, you want your staff to work as one team but also encourage them to form separate mini groups, because smaller groups exercise greater influence over their members. It's not by chance that the basic operating unit of the SAS is four troopers.

■ Whenever possible encourage good-natured competition between the mini groups. To avoid things getting too serious offer a trophy of no particular value to the 'best team' each month.

■ Now that you know that productivity increases when managers talk to staff get out of your office and indulge in a bit of management by walking about *(see Theory 10)*. If possible get senior managers to talk to your staff. This is easily done. Instead of having a private briefing from your boss or director on the organisation's latest strategy ask them to brief you and your team together (always assuming that nothing confidential is involved). When they have left you can answer any questions that your team have.

■ Everyone wants to feel valued. We spend most of our waking life at work and we need to believe that it has a purpose. So treat people with respect, as intelligent individuals, and watch productivity grow.

QUESTIONS TO ASK

■ How much do I know about the people who work for me?

■ Do I encourage staff to talk to me about their ambitions and problems?

THEORY 5 URWICK'S TEN PRINCIPLES OF MANAGEMENT

Use the span of control principle to ensure that managers aren't overloaded and that all staff have individual support.

Lyndall Urwick worked in the armed forces, industry and management consultancy and it's clear that his views on management were influenced by his military service.

URWICK'S TEN PRINCIPLES ARE:

Continuity: The organisation's structure should be designed to ensure the organisation's survival.

Balance: The various teams and departments within an organisation should be kept in balance in terms of position and power.

Definition: All jobs and the duties that go with them must be clearly defined.

Specialisation: Each group should have one function.

The objective: Every organisation should have one overriding purpose.

Authority: Every group can only have one manager.

Correspondence: Managers must have the necessary authority to fulfil their responsibilities.

Coordination: Managers are responsible for organisation and coordination.

The span of control: A manager should not have direct line management responsibility for more than six or seven staff.

Responsibility: The manager must take responsibility for his/her staff.

HOW TO USE IT

- Work with other managers in your organisation to ensure that the organisation's structure is fit for purpose and that the allocation of resources between sections/departments is based on need, not political manoeuvring by managers. Failure to do this will lead to sub-optimisation.

- Define the duties and limits of initiative attached to each post.

- Where appropriate use specialisation to improve productivity.

- Align your objectives with those of the organisation. If you don't you will be constantly fighting a battle you can't win.

- Avoid the situation where you share responsibility for staff with another manager. If reporting lines are unclear then sort them out *(see Theory 1)*.

- Before accepting a job check that you have the authority to meet your responsibilities. For example, if you have tight production deadlines do you have the last word on who is appointed to your team?

- You are responsible for the co-ordination and organisation of your staff and resources. Ensure that your team has the resources and systems they need to do their job *(see Theory 1)*.

- The introduction of flatter, less hierarchical structures means fewer managers and more people reporting to them. But people want to be treated as individuals. Use the span of control and work through six trusted lieutenants. They can each closely manage six people. Now 42 people are being given individualised attention. Go one level lower and it's 258.

- You're responsible for everything that goes on in your team. Take responsibility and staff will trust and respect you.

QUESTIONS TO ASK

- Do I spend too much time doing 'my work' rather than managing staff?

- How good am I at communicating with the staff under my control? Do I really know what is going on?

THEORY 6 DRUCKER ON THE FUNCTIONS OF MANAGEMENT (CROWN AS KING)

Use as your foundational management beliefs. Everything you do should flow from these fundamental statements. All else is embroidery.

Many people believe that Peter Drucker was the first true genius that the study of management produced. He helped establish the discipline of management and foresaw numerous trends in management many years in advance of anyone else. For example, he wrote about decentralisation in the 1940s, coined the term 'the knowledge economy' in 1969 and was talking about the social responsibilities of managers in the 1970s.

It was Drucker who in plain English suggested that the purpose of every business organisation was to create and maintain a customer. He didn't talk about maximising profits. He knew that only by building and maintaining customers can a business hope to make a profit, because it's customers that create profits.

DRUCKER ALSO ARGUED THAT MANAGERS WERE RESPONSIBLE FOR:

Setting the organisation's/team's objectives.

Providing and organising the resources required to achieve the objectives.

Motivating staff to achieve the objectives.

Monitoring staff performance against the objectives.

Improving performance by continually developing themselves and their staff.

Drucker's insights into the purpose of a business and the responsibilities of managers encapsulates the essence of both business and management theory.

HOW TO USE IT

- Identify who your customers are. Ask yourself: Who buys my goods or services? If you deal with the public this may be obvious, but if you provide a service to other parts of your organisation it may be more difficult.

- Once you have identified your customers ask: Am I meeting their needs? What can I do to enhance the service or product I provide? *(see Section 8)*. Based upon your answers develop a plan to provide customers with the best possible service.

- Provide targets and objectives for all staff. Set 80% of the targets at a level that is relatively easy for staff to achieve. This will turn people on to success and motivate them to meet the more challenging targets *(see Theory 88)*.

- Monitor performance. Establish a reporting system that shows performance against target, explains the reason for any discrepancies and is produced in time for you to take corrective action quickly.

- Constantly monitor the physical and staffing resources that you need to achieve your targets and take action to remedy any shortfalls before they become a problem.

- Motivate and communicate with your staff by sharing information and listening to what they have to say *(see Section 3)*.

- You are your own greatest asset. Invest time and energy in developing both your technical and managerial skills. Keep yourself marketable. Attend interviews regularly and if asked to define management or the role of managers trot out Drucker's list of management responsibilities as if they were your own. Your staff are your second greatest asset so develop, train and support them.

QUESTIONS TO ASK

- Do I really think of myself as a manager and act accordingly?
- Do I see my job in terms of the work I do or helping others do their job?

THEORY 7 McGREGOR'S X AND Y THEORY

Use to identify which stereotypical type of manager you are closest to and consider how this impacts on your actions and how you are perceived by staff.

Douglas McGregor identified two different sets of assumptions made by managers about their staff. Each set of assumptions represents an extreme view of people and can be summarised as follows:

Theory X managers believe that most people ...		Theory Y managers believe that most people ...
Are driven by monetary concerns	⟷	Are driven by job satisfaction
Will avoid work when possible	⟷	Actively seek work
Lack ambition and dislike responsibility	⟷	Show ambition and seek responsibility
Are indifferent to organisational needs	⟷	Are commited to organisational objectives
Lack creativity and resist change	⟷	Are creative and welcome change

McGregor believes that every manager's actions are governed by how they view human nature. A Theory X manager will attempt to exercise tight control by close supervision, demands for strict adherence to rules and threats of punishment. A Theory Y manager will create an environment where effort is recognised and rewarded and praise is given regularly.

HOW TO USE IT

■ Don't assume that modern managers should embrace Theory Y and disregard Theory X. In the real world you may have to deal with people whose only motivation is to earn as much money as possible for the least amount of effort.

■ Recognise that if you choose Theory X your style will be about command, control and fear and that you will rely on coercion *(see Theory 17)*, implicit threats and tight supervision to manage your staff. Do you want this?

■ If you choose Theory Y you will promote cooperation, rewards and good working relationships. But how are you going to deal with those members of staff who see such an approach as weakness?

■ Adopt an approach that lies somewhere between the two extremes of X and Y but recognise that there is a danger in switching between them. Staff expect managers to be consistent *(see Theory 12)*. Switching approaches may cause confusion.

■ To avoid confusion set clear limits for staff actions. Identify those rules, procedures and deadlines where you expect total compliance. Make it clear what failure to comply will mean and enforce your rules consistently.

■ Manage your team's remaining activities using a Theory Y inspired approach. Make yourself available to staff, listen to what they have to say and recognise that sometimes staff need you to believe in them before they can do their best work.

■ Always maintain basic ground rules. They keep you and the organisation safe from ne'er-do-wells who just want to take you for a ride.

QUESTIONS TO ASK

■ On a continuum, where Theory X is 1 and Theory Y is 100, where would you place yourself? On the same continuum, where would your staff place you?

■ Given your organisation's culture *(see Section 5)* how acceptable is your approach?

THEORY 8   PETERS AND WATERMAN'S THEORY OF MANAGEMENT

Use as a strategy to raise your organisation's performance by listening to your customers and frontline staff.

Tom Peters and Robert Waterman wrote the mega hit *In Search of Excellence*. Their aim was to identify the key features of excellent organisations. In later books Peters expanded on these ideas.

TO ACHIEVE SUCCESS AND REMAIN SUCCESSFUL ORGANISATIONS MUST:

Use transformational leadership *(see Theories 20–22)* to inspire and motivate staff. For this to work managers and staff must share a common set of values and act with integrity.

Listen to the customers and frontline staff, as often managers are too remote to know what customers think, feel or want.

Recognise that product innovation and improved working practices often come from frontline staff. Such staff should be recognised and celebrated, not ignored or marginalised as often happens.

Celebrate the organisation's history and build a shared organisational culture using its achievements, past events, stories and symbols as raw material (*see Section 5*).

Challenge bureaucracy wherever it grows and create pockets of excellence.

Encourage managers to be proactive, with a bias towards taking action, rather than reacting to events.

Use a loose–tight approach when exercising staff control. This allows staff to exercise their judgement within clearly defined parameters.

Stick to what they know and understand.

HOW TO USE IT

■ Peters and Waterman promote a state of mind rather than a single theory. If you like their ideas you need to think as they do and listen to frontline staff and customers *(see Theory 10)*.

■ Work with staff to develop a set of shared values and vision for your team *(see Theories 20–22)*. This is not easy and won't happen overnight. Start by asking: Why are we here? What's our purpose? Then take it from there.

■ At every opportunity listen to what customers say. Don't become defensive. Take on board their complaints and comments and work out what can be done to improve the situation *(see Section 8)*.

■ Build good lines of communication with frontline staff, listen to what they say and act upon it. Use them to identify opportunities for innovation. If an idea works share the credit for success with them. That way more ideas will flow in.

■ With the same passion as a member of the Spanish Inquisition seek out and destroy areas of bureaucracy in your organisation and build pockets of excellence.

■ Use spare time to find problems and deal with them before they can grow.

■ Just as you want to exercise your discretion, allow staff space to explore their own ideas. Don't yank too hard on the lead when they reach the limits of their discretion.

■ Stick to what you know. Don't get involved in work you don't understand unless you are willing to learn about the issues involved. In the late 1990s Warren Buffet was ridiculed for not investing in the burgeoning technology sector because, as he said, 'I don't understand these businesses'. By 2002, after the Dot Com Bubble had burst, he was seen as a genius.

QUESTIONS TO ASK

■ Is the organisation's culture compatible with Peters and Waterman's ideas?

■ Given my position how much of Peters and Waterman's approach to management can I adopt?

THEORY 9   COVEY'S SEVEN HABITS™ OF HIGHLY EFFECTIVE PEOPLE

Use to identify a strategy for reaching your own aims and objectives and a philosophy for how you treat people along the way.

Stephen Covey's seven habits™ model can be split into personal and interpersonal habits.

PERSONAL HABITS – WORKING ON YOURSELF – ARE:

Be proactive: Managers should aim to shape the events and environment in which they work and not just sit back and wait for things to happen.

Start with the end in mind: Managers should identify what they want to achieve. Once identified they must avoid distractions and constantly work on activities that take them towards their goals.

Put first things first: Managers should prioritise those activities that will help them achieve their aims.

Sharpen the saw: Managers are human. They need time to rest and renew themselves and update their skills.

INTERPERSONAL HABITS – WORKING WITH OTHERS – ARE:

Think win–win: When dealing with staff, customers, suppliers and even competitors wise managers look for common ground and a solution that suits all parties.

Seek first to understand then try to be understood: Like doctors, managers should diagnose what the problem is before they prescribe the cure.

Synergise: Synergy occurs when the outcome is greater than the sum of the parts. A case of 2 + 2 = 5. Great teamwork can achieve this (see Section 4).

HOW TO USE IT

■ To be proactive get off your backside and work towards the achievement of your aims. Don't sit about waiting for things to happen. Look for opportunities to shape events and the environment you work in.

■ Start with the end in mind by identifying your aims. What do you really want from life? Think about your earliest ambitions. What did you want to do when you were at school or just starting work? Now is the time to make your dreams concrete. Record them on paper as short (1 year), medium (2 to 3 years) and long-term (over 3 years) aims and tick them off as you achieve them.

■ Put first things first and identify which work activities move you closer to achieving your aims. Sometimes you may have to do other work. That's OK. But get back to the important stuff asap.

■ Sharpen the saw reminds you to look after yourself. Find time to relax, enjoy some R and R and update your professional skills.

■ When you deal with staff, customers and even competitors seek first to understand what they are saying. By listening you will gain an insight into what they really want.

■ Once you understand their wants you can identify a win–win solution that satisfies all parties. This will build trust which leads to better outcomes when you deal with the same people in the future.

■ The relationships that you have established on a basis of mutual respect and fairness will release synergy rather than competition and improve future results beyond expectation.

QUESTIONS TO ASK

■ What do I want from life? What are my aims and ambitions?

■ How am I going to achieve my aims and ambitions? What's my plan?

THEORY 10   MANAGEMENT BY WALKING ABOUT (MBWA)

Use MBWA to avoid becoming detached from staff and what is going on in your organisation.

Like a lot of theories MBWA is something that good managers have been doing since Adam and Eve first expressed an interest in apples and it's impossible to identify where the idea originated. But it's probably fair to say that both Mark McCormack and Tom Peters helped to popularise it.

The theory is simple. To avoid becoming isolated and losing touch with staff and the day-to-day operations of the organisation managers must get out of their office and walk around the factory, shop, site or office, listen to staff and observe what is going on at first hand.

USE THE WALKS AS AN OPPORTUNITY TO:
Build trust and understanding with staff.
Listen to what staff have to say and take on board their work problems and ideas.
Look for examples of good practice that can be implemented elsewhere in the organisation.
Look for examples of bad practice and eliminate them.
Observe how other managers and supervisors interact with staff.
Improve your knowledge of the business, its staff and products.
Answer staff questions.
Get to know people personally and what motivates/demotivates them.

HOW TO USE IT

- Identify an aim for every walk you take. This may be to find out what staff think of new working procedures, identify a problem or good practice in a specific section, get a feel for staff morale generally and on rare occasions to promote a new initiative.

- Don't talk at staff. Listen more than you speak and ask staff for their ideas and views on work issues. Don't be afraid to spend a few minutes talking about football or what was on telly last night if that helps the person to relax and open up.

- Always deliver on any promises that you make and never commit to anything you can't deliver.

- Once back in the office jot down a few notes on what you found and analyse your data into three categories, i.e.

  1 Matters that require immediate action.

  2 Information that will inform your future actions.

  3 Factual information about the organisation and its processes that you were unaware of.

- Use the data collected to improve the organisation's behaviours, practices and processes and to inform your decisions.

QUESTIONS TO ASK

- When was the last time I 'walked the job'?

- Where does your information about the business come from? How many filters has it gone through before it reaches me?

A FINAL WORD ON MANAGEMENT THEORIES

WHY DRUCKER'S THEORY WAS CROWNED KING

When Einstein submitted his six-page PhD thesis his examiners were impressed with his ideas but asked him to 'write a little more'. He took it away, thought about it for a week, added one sentence and resubmitted his thesis. It passed.

A theory doesn't have to be long and complicated to be profound. Drucker summarises the purpose of a business and the role of managers in under 75 words. Yet these few words have been the basis for much of the management thinking and writing for the past 60 years. And he didn't even have to add an extra sentence.

The most consistent message that comes across in this section is that management theories are often contradictory. I mean, writers can't even decide if it's better to batter staff into submission with a blunt instrument or wrap them in cotton wool. But that's OK because as I said in the Introduction people and situations are infinitely variable and you can't expect one approach to be successful in every situation or with every person.

Always remember that you're a manager not an administrator. Your job is to organise and coordinate the work of your staff, not fill in forms. If you're new to management you must act, think and talk like a manager (and no, I don't mean spouting all that ridiculous management-speak which makes me want to run the idiot using it up the nearest flag pole just to see who salutes). You are no longer a member of staff or an administrator, you're a manager. So manage.

As a manager you are responsible for achieving results by setting objectives, organising resources, motivating staff, monitoring performance and developing people including yourself. That's the job and you can't run away from it. So get stuck in and start managing.

If you're a new manager the quickest way to make an impact is to look for ways to improve the efficiency and effectiveness of your team. Embrace new technologies and don't be slow to pinch good ideas from competitors or another team *(see Theory 74)*. If anyone tells you that they do a job in a particular way because 'that's how it's always been done' you know that you have found a process that is ripe for change.

If you are an established manager then explore the limits of your power and authority. Most managers underestimate just how much power they have *(see Theories 74 and 75)*. Take it out for a spin and see where it takes you. Remember, it's always easier to apologise than to ask for permission if you overstep the mark, provided you don't do a Nick Gleeson and bankrupt the organisation.

If you have just moved up from a middle to a senior management no one is likely to tell you the limits of your power or responsibilities, so push the boundaries. As a senior manager that's what people expect you to do. You weren't appointed because you're a shrinking violet.

Whatever stage your management career has reached remember that staff need clarity. So avoid ambiguity and uncertainty and ensure that staff know exactly who they report to and what is expected of them. Leave no room for doubt.

Never forget that you achieve results through people. Therefore build a good working relationship with all your staff. Treat everyone equally and judge them on their actions and not how much you like or dislike them. As a manager you can't afford to have favourites. It causes resentment and jealousy in the team and reduces productivity.

Listen to staff and customers. Amongst the odd moan and gripe will be some real nuggets of wisdom. Your job is to sift the gold from the dross. To do this you need to keep an open mind, one that is looking for clever and unusual ideas. Can you imagine Sir Walter Raleigh's reception in the taverns of London when he first suggested that we put tobacco leaves in our mouth and set fire to them? Who would have thought that his idea would spawn a multi-billion pound industry? Consult with your staff about any problems that have been reported to you, as they may have the answer sitting on their desk just waiting to be implemented.

By all means help colleagues, who knows when you will need a favour from them, but don't let their crises derail your work. Learn to be assertive and don't accept the responsibility for the work or mistakes of other people unless they are members of your team.

When you are at work, work hard. When you are away from work play hard but find time to relax. You're not a machine. Be kind to yourself; no one else will – except maybe your dog, family and true friends (in that order). Keep up-to-date with developments in your area of work/ profession and attend at least one job interview a year even if you don't want to change jobs. That way you'll retain your match fitness, discover what's going on, have a good idea of your market value and be well prepared when it's time to move on.

Finally, remember: you have two ears and one mouth; clever managers use them in that proportion.

SECTION 2

HOW TO LEAD PEOPLE

INTRODUCTION

So what is leadership? The word lead means 'to guide on a way by going in advance' (*Longman New Universal Dictionary*). So it's safe to say that leading involves taking someone on a journey from their current position to somewhere else. The journey can be physical as when Moses led the Israelites out of Egypt or psychological as where a leader turns around the attitudes of a group of workers. Whichever it is, it involves change. You can't be a leader unless you lead change of some kind. That's what leaders do, they change things.

Unfortunately we've all experienced leaders who change things just to enhance their CV. They implement a major change and then leave before the effects of their actions kick in and they get blamed for another monumental cock-up. Good leaders always have a purpose in mind when they make a change and the best leaders will only make changes that help the organisation achieve its objectives.

But how does the leader bring about change? They can't do it on their own. They need the help of others. This turns leadership into a process which involves influencing others to work towards the achievement of your aims and objectives. Leadership is not about power or force, it's about influence. You don't want an army of conscripts as followers; you want an army of volunteers.

The entries in this section are largely in chronological order but only trait theory predates 1930. Some you will be familiar with, such as Hersey and Blanchard's situational leadership; others, like leader member exchange, may be new to you.

In recent years, transformational leadership (TL) has become the leadership style of choice for many organisations. For that reason, and because of how the theory evolved in three phases, I've used three entries to explore this important theory. This means that you need to read the entries on Burns, Bass and Bennis and Nanus to get a complete picture of how to use this theory.

Whichever theory or theories you decide to adopt there is one characteristic you must exhibit at all times if you are to convince people that you are worth following, and that is self-confidence. If you lack faith in your own abilities or the leadership approach that you adopt why should anyone place their trust in you? It's essential that you always appear self-confident and optimistic – especially when you're terrified. To achieve this 'Act as if yea have faith and faith will be given to you', or in other words always act with confidence and before long the act will become reality. Besides, it's not how you feel that is important, it's how you are perceived by your staff/followers that matters.

Many great leaders have been wracked with nerves and self-doubt. Indeed it's probably only the mad and megalomaniacs who are free from doubt. Good leaders face their fears and triumph over them. You can do the same. Besides, if being a leader was easy everyone would be doing it. It's the challenge that makes it worth doing.

THEORY 11 TRAIT THEORY

Use to identify the key traits that you need to exhibit consistently if you wish to be considered a leader.

The origins of trait theory are unknown but its purpose is simple. It tries to identify the innate characteristics that distinguish leaders from followers. Unfortunately, over a century of research has failed to reveal a definitive list of traits that all leaders possess. Despite this failure the theory remains popular because people retain a romantic attachment to the idea that leaders are a special breed and have innate characteristics that make them worth following. Anyone who wishes to be considered a leader will need to display several if not all of the following traits.

POPULAR TRAITS THAT LEADERS ARE EXPECTED TO DISPLAY INCLUDE:

Self-confidence.

Social skills.

Motivational skills.

Integrity.

Responsibility.

Intelligence.

Helicopter behaviour.

Sector-specific traits may also be required, e.g. in the armed forces, police or fire service physical courage is important while in a university academic ability is essential.

HOW TO USE IT

- Look for opportunities to demonstrate to your staff and boss that you have the necessary traits to be a leader.

- Exhibit self-confidence at all times – especially when you're terrified. How you feel is immaterial. It's how you are perceived that counts.

- You don't have to be a great talker to be sociable. In any conversation encourage others to talk and actively listen. Do this and people will think you're highly sociable and you'll pick up valuable information.

- To motivate staff lead by example, show enthusiasm for your team's work and find ways to make staff feel proud of their work *(see Section 3)*.

- People follow those they trust, so act with integrity and demonstrate that you won't sacrifice any member of staff on the altar of your own ambition.

- Accept responsibility for the errors that you and your team make. Don't blame others. Passing the buck is not allowed.

- You need a certain level of intelligence to be a leader. But people seldom follow a genius because they don't believe that a genius could understand their problems. President Clinton has a genius level IQ but when talking to the public he liked to appear as just another 'good old boy'. It won him a lot of votes.

- When considering a problem or making a decision rise like a helicopter above the narrow interests of your own team and make decisions based upon what is best for the entire organisation. Do this consistently and you will be noticed.

- Identify and demonstrate any sector-specific traits that are relevant.

QUESTION TO ASK

- How can I get a clear picture of how staff, colleagues and management see me. How can I build on the positives and eliminate the negatives that my appraisal has thrown up?

THEORY 12 # THE MICHIGAN AND OHIO STUDIES – BASIC STYLE THEORY

Use to identify your default leadership style – i.e. are you a task- or person-oriented leader?

In the 1940s the University of Michigan suggested that leadership behaviour could be described as either person or task oriented. Person-oriented leaders are concerned with maintaining good relationships with staff and believe in a participative and democratic approach to leadership.

Task-oriented leaders are more concerned with results and outputs than people's feelings. They are target driven, directive and controlling. They seldom listen to staff.

Michigan University depicted these two archetypes as residing at the opposite ends of a single continuum. This implied that leaders could only be concerned with people or achievement of task but not both.

Ohio University developed the basic theory and argued that employee and task orientation did not reside on a single continuum but on two separate continua each of which ran from low to high. This meant that it was possible for a leader to have one of four leadership styles.

The leadership styles available to a leader are:

- a high concern for staff and task;
- a high concern for staff and a low concern for task;
- a low concern for both staff and task;
- a low concern for staff and a high concern for task.

High		
Concern for task	Managers are only concerned with getting the job done	Managers are concerned for their staff and getting the job done
	Managers have no concern for staff or task	Managers concerned with staff relations but have little interest in getting the job done
Low		High

Concern for staff

HOW TO USE IT

- If you currently emphasise getting the job done over concern for staff, don't abandon your drive and passion for performance but add to it a concern for the staff's well-being.

- Improve your relationships with staff by taking the time to get to know them. Chat with them for a couple of minutes before you get down to business. You will be amazed at how much this will improve the atmosphere at work.

- Involve staff in discussions about how work is scheduled and organised as a means of getting them to own targets and become self-monitoring *(see Section 3)*.

- If you currently emphasise the needs of staff over getting the job done ask yourself: Do I get enough productivity out of my staff? If the answer is 'no' move towards a more task-oriented approach.

- Start by recognising that you are not the staff's friend, councillor or shrink. You are their manager and although you can be friendly with them you are paid to ensure that they do their job.

- Set a small number of key targets and deadlines for all staff and insist that they be met. Once these have been accepted build upon them until you have an equal concern for both staff and task.

- Aim to act in a firm, fair, friendly and supportive manner at all times. There will be occasions when you have to demand maximum effort from staff. But people aren't stupid. They know when a job is important or urgent and if you have a good relationship with them they won't want to let you down.

- If you have no interest in the task or your staff get out of management.

QUESTIONS TO ASK

- Do I lack the confidence to be directive and give orders when required? Or do I appear aggressive to staff?
- Do I need assertiveness training?

THEORY 13 BLAKE AND MOUTON'S LEADERSHIP GRID®

Use to confirm your preferred leadership style while recognising that you can change your style as circumstances require.

Blake and Mouton built upon basic style theory *(see Theory 12)* and produced their Leadership Grid. The grid identifies how much concern the leader has for getting the job done (task-centred) and for their staff (person-centred). They identified five leadership styles.

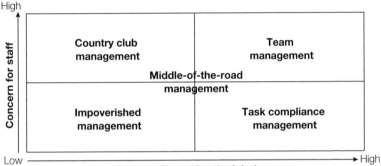

Source: Adapted from Northouse, P. G., *Leadership: Theory and Practice* (4th edn) (Grid International, Inc., 2006).

- **Country club management:** Leader has little interest in task completion but a high concern for the social needs of staff.
- **Task compliance management:** Leader has little concern for staff's needs. Their overwhelming concern is with achievement of task/ targets.
- **Middle-of-the road management:** Leader is content to compromise. They seek to satisfy rather than maximise both the well-being of staff and production.
- **Impoverished management:** Leader has very little interest in either staff or task. They do the bare minimum to get by.
- **Team management:** Leader emphasises both the need for high levels of achievement and excellent staff relations. Blake and Mouton suggest that this is the approach all leaders should use.

HOW TO USE IT

- Complete Blake and Mouton's leadership questionnaire (available online). This will identify your default leadership style.
- If you're a team manager, great. But beware. You need to appear committed and caring not frantic and fawning.
- If you're a country club manager this approach may be appropriate after a particularly tough period of work, but it can't continue indefinitely. You must eventually place greater emphasis on task completion (see Theory 12).
- If you're a middle-of-the-road manager Blake and Mouton will tell you that this approach has little merit. But is it realistic to expect staff to consistently work flat out? An approach that produces work levels in the 80–90% range, with an ability to perform at the 90%+ level when required may be a good strategy for longevity. Only you can decide if this is an acceptable approach in your organisation.
- If you're a task manager with an emphasis on getting the job done then your approach will be clearly appropriate in periods of crisis or extreme pressure. However, if used as your default position you should aim to achieve a better balance between a concern for work and people (see Theory 12).
- If you are an impoverished manager you are either in the wrong organisation and you need to change jobs or you have no interest in management, in which case you need to change careers.
- Recognise that a single style will not work in every situation. Therefore remain flexible and adapt your management style to changing circumstances.

QUESTIONS TO ASK

- Which leadership style is used by the most respected/successful leaders in my organisation?
- Does my leadership style reflect or clash with the most popular style in the organisation?

THEORY 14
ADAIR'S ACTION-CENTRED LEADERSHIP

Use to remind you that you have to continually balance the needs of the task, the team and the individual and that on occasions you will have to emphasise the needs of one over the other two.

John Adair's model contains elements of both style and contingency theory *(see Theories 12 and 15)*. He emphasises that a leader must constantly balance the needs of the task, the individual and the team but he recognises that at certain times the needs of one may have to supersede the other two.

Manager's area of responsibility

Source: Adapted from Adair, J., *John Adair's Greatest Ideas for Being a Brilliant Manager* (Capstone, 2011).

- **Individual needs:** Include meeting the coaching, mentoring and motivation needs of staff.
- **Group needs:** Include training, team building, motivating and maintaining discipline of the group.
- **Task needs:** Include setting work standards, deadlines, targets and providing the resources required to do the job.

HOW TO USE IT

- Where the needs of the person, team and task clash, base your decision about which area to prioritise by reference to what is best for the organisation in the long term. The organisation employs you to take decisions in its best interest, not those of any group or individual in the organisation.

- Where the need of the person conflicts with the team, base your decision on what is best for the team. This default position recognises that when anyone joins a team they sign up to the unwritten law that they must subordinate their needs to the good of the team.

- The above approaches are underpinned by the old maxim that decisions should be based on the greatest good for the greatest number of people. If you are happy with this approach it's not a bad default position to start from.

- Be aware that there will always be exceptions to the approach outlined above where the need of an individual or team rightly trumps those of the task and organisation.

- If your decision angers an individual or team don't let the grievance fester. Talk to the aggrieved party and explain the reasons for your decision. They may still disagree with your decision but they will be happy that they had the opportunity to voice their anger *(see Theory 83).*

QUESTIONS TO ASK

- Which set of needs do I generally prioritise?
- How difficult have I found it to vary my default position?

THEORY 15 FIEDLER'S CONTINGENCY THEORY

Use to assess how favourable or unfavourable your situation is and identify which factors you need to address to improve the situation.

Fred Fiedler's contingency theory tries to match leaders to posts in which they will be successful. It's called contingency theory because it suggests that a leader's effectiveness will be contingent upon how well their style of leadership fits the post they hold.

THE FAVOURABLENESS OF THE POST IS ASSESSED USING THREE FACTORS:

The relationship between the leader and their followers. Is it good, bad or indifferent?

The level of structure in the work undertaken by the followers. For example, work in any fast food chain is highly structured with written instructions on how to complete every process. Compare that to a marketing manager for an arts organisation who is given wide discretion in how to do their job – low structure.

The positional power of the leader. That is, to what extent the leader can punish or reward followers?

Taken together the above factors describe how favourable the situation is to the leader. Fiedler argues that situations are most favourable when there are good leader/follower relations, the task is well defined and there is strong leadership position power. Situations are unfavourable when leader/staff relationships are poor, the task is unstructured and the leader has weak positional power.

HOW TO USE IT

- Use contingency theory to analyse your position and identify the source of any problems you face. Is it the staff, the nature of the work, your lack of power or a combination of all three that is the problem? Once you have identified the problem, devise a course of action to resolve the issue.

- Often it's just one person that is the problem. Usually, they see themselves as the unofficial leader of the team and are afraid of losing their power. Either win them over or, if that fails, use all your powers to bring them into line *(see Theories 76 and 77)*. But once you start such a struggle you have to win. Lose and you are finished.

- If it's the nature of the work that makes it difficult to control the actions of staff, establish procedures that require them to report to you regularly on their progress/performance. Also set clear limits to the discretion they can exercise.

- Power is seldom given to you, you have to take it. So use the power/ authority that comes with your position to sort the problem out. Few will dispute your right to use it *(see Theories 76 and 77)*.

- Contingency theory suggests that when you find yourself in an unfavourable situation you should change the situation not your leadership approach. You may decide that in many situations it is quicker and easier to change your leadership approach *(see Theories 7, 12, 13 and 17)*.

QUESTIONS TO ASK

- Is there a single person or issue that is the source of the problems I face?

- Is the job for me? It may genuinely be the case that you are not suited to this particular post. If so, get out.

THEORY 16 # HERSEY AND BLANCHARD'S SITUATIONAL LEADERSHIP THEORY (CROWN AS KING)

Use with staff every time you give them a new task to perform.

If you've ever been on a middle managers' leadership course there is a good chance that you are familiar with Ken Blanchard's and Paul Hersey's situational leadership theory. It's widely used by trainers and popular with managers because it provides clear advice on how to lead staff.

The basic theory suggests that, as a leader, you need to provide a combination of direction and support when dealing with a member of staff. Direction involves giving the person detailed instructions on how to complete the task/job, i.e. telling them how to do the job. Support requires you to provide the encouragement and personal support that they need to complete the task/job, i.e. telling them that you believe they can do the job.

THE FOUR APPROACHES THAT YOU CAN ADOPT ARE:

Coaching: where you provide high levels of both direction and support.

Directing: where you provide high levels of direction but low levels of support.

Supporting: where you provide high levels of support but low levels of direction.

Delegating: where you provide low levels of support and low levels of direction.

It is important to note that followers do not progress through the model from directing to delegating in a linear fashion. As each new task is delegated the role of the leader is to identify what type of support, if any, the member of staff requires to successfully complete the new task.

HOW TO USE IT

■ To use situational theory effectively you need to know and understand the people who work for you. Start collecting that information now!

■ Identify the task that you want completed.

■ Use your knowledge of the staff, their experience, existing workload and priorities to select a person to do the job. Let's call that person Charlie.

■ Make an initial judgement as to which of the four approaches you will use with Charlie.

■ Discuss with Charlie what needs to be done. Encourage them to ask questions and identify what information or support is needed from you to do the job.

■ Use open and closed questions to assess how well Charlie understands the task and how confident they feel about completing the job.

■ Based on the answers decide if your initial judgement about Charlie's suitability for the task was correct. If in doubt err on the side of caution and select an approach which allows for additional support to be provided if required.

■ Delegate the task and provide a deadline for completion. Monitor progress. If required, schedule regular meetings to discuss progress. Where a delegating approach has been used such meetings may only last a couple of minutes. But where a directing approach has been used they may last much longer.

■ Regardless of which approach is used make it clear to Charlie that if any problems arises you are available to help.

■ On successful completion thank Charlie for the work and use the two most motivational words available to any leader: 'Well done' *(see Section 3)*.

■ This approach can also be used when dealing with an entire team *(see Section 4)*.

QUESTIONS TO ASK

■ How good am I at delegating? Do I only delegate to one or two trusted people?

■ Have I the courage/confidence to trust my staff?

THEORY 17 # BURNS' TRANSACTIONAL LEADERSHIP THEORY

Use to obtain compliance from a member of staff who needs to be persuaded to comply with your request.

It was James MacGregor Burns who popularised the phrase 'transactional leadership'. In doing so he described a process that has been going on between leaders and followers, managers and staff and parents and children since Adam was a lad in short pants.

Burns' theory describes the, often informal, bartering process that goes on between leaders and staff all the time. He identified two very different strategies that managers can use.

Constructive transactions occur:	Corrective or coercive transactions occur:
When the leader offers inducements to the follower to comply with their request. For example, 'If you work tonight you can have Friday afternoon off.'	When the leader threatens the follower if they refuse to co-operate or if they fail to stop acting in a certain way. For example, 'If you do that again I'll make sure you get no overtime for the next month.'

Burns believed that the range of inducements and threats available to a leader were virtually limitless and were not restricted to financial rewards or sanctions (*see Theory 26*).

HOW TO USE IT

■ Confirm the limits of your power/authority *(see Theories 74 and 75)*. As a leader your ability to deliver on what you promise or threaten is vital. You must deliver on both or you'll lose credibility.

■ Find out what makes your staff tick. It's alright reading about the various factors that either motivate or demotivate followers *(see Section 3)*. But every individual is different. You need to identify specifically what your followers really value and fear and use this knowledge in your negotiations.

■ This data-gathering exercise must be on-going. It starts on the day you arrive and only finishes when you move on to a new job.

■ Start with constructive transactions. A willing volunteer is always better than some poor sod that has been coerced into doing a job.

QUESTIONS TO ASK

■ If I constantly engage in constructive transactions will staff see me as a soft touch and/or expect rewards for everything they do?

■ What effect will the use of coercive transactions have on levels of co-operation and team spirit?

THEORY 18 # DANSEREAU, GRAEN AND HAGA'S LEADER MEMBER EXCHANGE (LMX) THEORY

Use if you wish to (potentially) develop a close working relationship with every member of your team and ensure their loyalty to you and you alone.

Dansereau, Graen and Haga's theory is unusual in that it both describes what leaders do and suggests a strategy for how they should act. LMX suggests that the leader should try to establish a close working relationship with each follower individually.

TO ACHIEVE THIS LEADERS FOLLOW A THREE-STAGE PROCESS:

Stage 1 – the stranger phase: At this stage the relationship is one of manager/employee. The relationship is defined by the person working to their job description and the leader watching for signs of potential.

Stage 2 – the acquaintance phase: If potential is identified the leader invites the person to take on additional work and responsibilities. During this phase the leader assesses if the worker has what it takes to become a full member of the in-group.

Stage 3 – the mature partnership phase: If the leader is satisfied with the person's performance they are invited to join the in-group. In return for taking on additional responsibilities and showing loyalty to the leader they gain greater access to the leader, more interesting work and opportunities for training and advancement.

Those not in the in-group are in the out-group.

The strength of LMX theory is that it allows a leader to build a strong and loyal follower base. The followers' commitment and loyalty improves productivity and team cohesion and targets and objectives are achieved more quickly and with less hassle *(see Section 4)*.

HOW TO USE IT

■ Decide if you wish to use LMX. Many people feel that it is an unethical form of leadership. However, provided all staff are given the same opportunity to join the in-group LMX isn't inherently unfair.

■ Identify what you can offer staff in return for working harder and showing greater commitment and loyalty to you. It might be access, a reputation for having the ear of the leader or greater opportunities to discuss their views and ideas.

■ Do not announce that you are going to adopt a form of LMX leadership or advertise the benefits of being in the in-group. Instead demonstrate through your actions with individual members of staff the benefits that are on offer. Other staff will quickly realise what is going on.

■ Almost certainly, you will be able identify some staff who are already working above what is expected of them. Start with them. Then work outwards.

■ As staff begin to recognise the benefits of in-group membership many will want to join. Ensure that everyone gets the same chance to join but only recruit those who have demonstrated by their attitude to work that they are willing to enter into a closer working relationship.

■ You are not being unfair if you refuse membership to someone who lacks commitment to their work but it is unfair to exclude someone just because you don't like them.

QUESTIONS TO ASK

■ Can I be confident that my in-group will not just be made up of friends?

■ How am I going to deal with the members of my out-group?

THEORY 19 # HOUSE'S CHARISMATIC LEADERSHIP THEORY

Use to remind you that you should constantly act as a role model for your followers, even if you aren't particularly charismatic.

Charismatic leadership has been around for a long time but it was Robert House who established it in the popular imagination during the 1970s. He sees charisma as a particularly powerful personality trait that only a few people have and which marks them out as leaders in the minds of many. Typically charismatic leaders and their followers demonstrate the following characteristics:

CHARISMATIC LEADERS

ACT AS A ROLE MODEL FOR THEIR FOLLOWERS

Promote an ideology based upon their moral beliefs.

Display beliefs and values that followers are attracted to and wish to adopt as their own.

Demonstrate integrity and competence to their followers.

Exhibit confidence in their followers to overcome obstacles and achieve 'great things'.

Consciously build up the self-belief and competence of followers.

FOLLOWERS OF CHARISMATIC LEADERS

DEMONSTRATE TRUST AND BELIEF IN THEIR LEADER'S IDEOLOGY

Show loyalty and obedience to the leader.

Identify with the leader and his/her goals.

See the leader as a person who deserves their love, gratitude and respect.

The result of this close relationship between leader and followers is that people become part of a collective identity with a common aim and purpose. Followers express themselves and find fulfilment by working towards their leader's objectives and trying to please him/her.

HOW TO USE IT

- Remember charisma is in the eye of the beholder, you don't have to possess it for others to think you have it.

- Be honest and assess how much charisma you think you have. This is tough. It's like finally realising that you'll never play for West Bromwich Albion. But the truth is you probably don't have a lot of charisma in the terms that House or Weber *(see Theory 76)* use. But that doesn't mean you can't apply aspects of charismatic theory.

- Identify your principles. This is difficult. The easiest way to start is to ask the question: What issue/s would I be willing to resign over? Any other 'so-called principles' are just positions you take until they become inconvenient and you change them.

- Act as a role model for your staff. Display your beliefs, principles and values through your actions. Don't preach; instead demonstrate good humour, honesty, fairness, punctuality, a willingness to listen, hard work and loyalty to your staff and they will respect you.

- Follow the Golden Rule and 'treat others as you would like to be treated'. Do this and you will win hearts and minds and be trusted by staff, colleagues and senior managers. Acting with integrity doesn't mean you're a soft touch. It's always easier to go with the flow than to stand up for your principles.

- Most people lack self-confidence *(see Theory 11)*. Staff need someone to believe in them. Provide that belief and staff will both admire and surprise you.

QUESTIONS TO ASK

- Who do I think is a charismatic leader? What characteristics do they have that I admire?

- Do I have those same characteristics or could I develop them?

THEORY 20 # BURNS' TRANSFORMATIONAL LEADERSHIP (TL) THEORY

Use as a means of energising your staff by aligning their goals with yours and those of the organisation.

James MacGregor Burns provided the basic transformational theory which was later expanded upon by Bass *(see Theory 21)* and Bennis and Nanus *(see Theory 22)*. To understand the developed theory and how to use it you should read this and the following two entries.

Burns was a political sociologist who was interested in how politicians attracted and energised their followers/voters. He identified two types of political leadership behaviour. Transactional politicians promised people something in return for voting for them, e.g. tax cuts *(see Theory 17)*. Whereas transformational politicians appealed to the voter's higher order wants and needs, e.g. Obama's 'Yes we can' slogan *(see Theory 23)*.

Burns' fundamental insight was that:

> ... before a leader can appeal to people's higher order needs they must identify and understand the beliefs, dreams and ambitions of the people. Only then can they package or mould their message to appeal to their target audience and followers.

Burns emphasises that genuine transformational relationships are not based on exploitation or manipulation, but on trust and integrity which increases the level of motivation and morality of both parties and leads to personal growth and development for all involved.

Burns believed that transformational leadership could be used with one person or thousands.

Transformational leadership deals with the relationship between leaders and followers in a way that no other theory does.

HOW TO USE IT

- Start by finding out what makes your staff tick if you want to use TL.

- Use MBWA *(see Theory 10)*, performance review meetings, team meetings, daily conversations and informal observations of staff to build up a picture of their personalities, interests, ambitions and beliefs.

- Identify common ambitions, beliefs, views and wants. If you manage a large staff you may have to use sampling to get a handle on these.

- Once you understand what your people want from work, package your message in a clear and unambiguous way which will allow them to make their own connections between your agenda and their own wants/needs.

- Remember the old advertising adage, 'most people don't know what they want until someone tells them'. As a transformational leader that's what you have to do, offer followers something that they have always wanted but only recognise when you present it to them.

QUESTIONS TO ASK

- If TL is used in my organisation, what do I need to do to align my team's aims with the organisation's mission and values?

- If TL is not used what aspects of it can I use with my team?

THEORY 21 **BASS AND TRANSFORMATIONAL LEADERSHIP (TL) THEORY**

Use to identify the values and beliefs that you need to display to be recognised as a transformational leader.

Bernard Bass built upon the work of Burns to develop an expanded and more detailed version of transformational leadership theory.

BASS IDENTIFIED WHAT HE CALLED THE 4Is:

Idealised influence refers to the charisma *(see Theory 19)*. It describes a leader who appears to be special, acts as a role model for followers and has strong ethical and moral values. Followers aspire to be like such leaders and want to follow them.

Inspirational motivation refers to how transformational leaders set high standards and expectations for their followers and demonstrate absolute confidence in the follower's ability to meet or exceed the targets set.

Intellectual stimulation describes how transformational leaders encourage their followers to question not only their beliefs and values but also those of the leader. Through this rigorous and open examination Bass believes that opportunities for personal growth, innovation and creativity are discovered.

Idealised consideration refers to how transformational leaders listen to the needs and problems of their followers and act as guide, mentor and coach with the aim of moving each follower closer to self-actualisation *(see Theory 23)*.

HOW TO USE IT

- Idealised influence is concerned with charisma *(see Theory 19)*. Regardless of how charismatic you are you must model good behaviour and strong ethical and moral values for your followers. Act as you speak. Treat all staff fairly and be honest in your dealings with everyone you come in contact with. Never sacrifice anyone to further your career. Do this and staff will respect you.

- Motivate staff *(see Section 3)* by setting high standards and show that you have faith in their ability to rise to any challenge. Everyone needs someone to believe in them. If you provide that belief staff will strain to meet your expectations. When they achieve they will remember that it was you that lit the blue touch-paper.

- Intellectual stimulation is a difficult concept for many leaders to embrace. It requires you to challenge your own views and beliefs. Be willing to accept good ideas wherever they come from and to accept criticism from staff when they challenge your ideas and suggestions. Don't be defensive when this happens; instead reflect on what has been said and decide if the criticisms are justified.

- With idealised consideration we are back to knowing your staff and responding to their needs, not just your own *(see Theories 17 and 20)*. Act as guide, mentor and coach with staff and they will blossom and grow to the benefit of the organisation.

QUESTIONS TO ASK

- How comfortable will I be if staff challenge my views and ideas?
- What strategies will I use to deal with such challenges?

THEORY 22 # BENNIS AND NANUS' TRANSFORMATIONAL LEADERSHIP (TL) THEORY

Use this to develop a vision for your organisation based on values and beliefs and not management-speak.

Following interviews with a range of leaders Warren Bennis and Burt Nanus identified four strategies that leaders should use when trying to transform their organisations. These are shown in the figure below.

STRATEGY 1	Develop a clear and understandable vision for the organisation
STRATEGY 2	Act as social architects for the organisation by changing the organisational culture
STRATEGY 3	Create trust throughout the organisation by making explicit their values and views
STRATEGY 4	Identify their own strengths and weaknesses and encourage their followers to do the same

HOW TO USE IT

■ Develop a clear vision for your team. Your vision has to be simple, understandable and worthwhile and unless you are running the organisation it must be aligned with the organisation's overall aims and objectives.

■ Decide if the existing organisational culture *(see Section 5)* supports or hinders the achievement of your vision. If it impedes it, and your vision is aligned with the organisation's, then you have every right to replace it with one that reflects the organisation's vision. Embarking on such a change requires careful planning *(see Section 6)*.

■ Create a bond of trust with your staff by making clear your values, views and position and stand by these even when the going gets tough. Such consistency of behaviour will increase the trust that people have in you which will make changing the organisational culture considerably easier.

■ Transformational leaders know their strengths and weaknesses. They display no false modesty or pride, they emphasise their strengths and use others to compensate for their weakness. You must do the same.

■ Play to your strengths and surround yourself with good people who are strong in those areas where you are weak. You are not showing weakness if you say 'I don't understand'. It's the idiot who pretends to understand and then reveals their ignorance with every word they say. Much like the chief executive I worked for in the public sector who didn't know the difference between cash and profit.

QUESTIONS TO ASK

■ Whose support do I need to bring about cultural and organisational change?

■ Who is likely to try and block cultural and organisational change and how do I deal with them?

A FINAL WORD ON LEADERSHIP THEORIES

WHY HERSEY AND BLANCHARD WERE CROWNED KING

Many theorists criticise Hersey and Blanchard because their theory has not been subject to rigorous academic research. So what? Situational theory has provided thousands of leaders with a simple and effective way to lead staff. Hersey and Blanchard's books have been best sellers worldwide and every year thousands of training events, based on their theory, are run. The theory has proved its value in the toughest research environment possible – the marketplace. It's easy to understand; easy to use and intuitively it feels and sounds right. Take it out for a spin and see what you think.

In any leadership situation there are two parties, the leader and their followers. The more you know about yourself and your followers the better leader you will be. In many ways it's easier to dig up information and insights on your followers, knowing ourselves is the hard bit. We don't even know what we look like because we have never seen a three-dimensional image of ourselves, so is it any surprise that we know even less about our personality and how we are perceived by other people. The only way to get an idea of what you are really like is to ask others. Use Johari windows theory *(see Theory 87)* to help you kick-start the process.

However, it's worth remembering that in management perception is reality. As a leader how you are perceived by followers is more important than how you feel. So identify how you want to be perceived and then act accordingly. The more you do this the quicker you will become the type of leader you want to be.

Your actual leadership style is determined by how you behave and it's always possible to change your behaviour. Even ingrained habits can be changed in about six weeks according to clinical psychologists. By all means identify and use a specific default management style but remain flexible and remember that circumstances change decisions/actions. You are free to adopt the most suitable style at any given time. This will require you to access and emphasise particular aspects of your character to meet the needs of the job. Using your full range of skills is not the same as being insincere. You may not like accessing your inner b******* but that characteristic is within you and sometimes it's required.

When dealing with staff, always remember that mutual benefit is a better basis for an on-going relationship than resentment and bubbling bile. In any transactional situation start by making a reasonable offer (constructive transactions) and only resort to sanctions (coercive transactions) as a last resort.

As a leader you should never base your judgements of staff on how they look, their gender, personality, how much you like/dislike them or who in the organisation they are related to. The only criterion should be how good they are at their job. This is particularly important if you adopt LMX theory *(see Theory 18)*. Of course if they do a great job but their personality drives the rest of the team to near violence you'll have to do something about it.

If you are a middle manager and want to use transformational leadership with your team you must align your agenda with the organisation's overall aims. If you fail to do so you'll find yourself fighting an uphill battle which can only ever have one winner.

Transformational leadership is based on integrity. Don't pretend to be something you're not. You will be found out. If you demonstrate integrity people will be drawn to you because they think that they can trust you. The quickest and easiest way to destroy their trust in you is to be hypocritical. How many politicians have made a career out of 'family values' only to be destroyed by revelations of three in a bed or taking the dog for a walk at midnight on the common? So never pretend to be something you're not.

Any vision you have for your team needs to be simple, clear, meaningful and explainable in one sentence. See if you can match NASA's. During the 1960s a Congressional Committee was visiting NASA and one of them asked a cleaner what his job was. Without missing a beat the cleaner replied, 'Putting a man on the moon'. Now that's a successful vision.

Every leader needs a certain amount of power and influence to drive through the changes they want to implement. You must be willing to use the full range of resources available to you to gain control of the situation *(see Theories 76, 77 and 78)*. The quickest, easiest and most legitimate way to access the power you need is to explicitly align your aims with the organisation's agenda. That way your actions are legitimised in the eyes of both your staff and the organisation's hierarchy.

Finally, as a leader you should always remember that if you stand for nothing you will be willing to stand for anything.

SECTION 3

HOW TO MOTIVATE YOUR STAFF

INTRODUCTION

Dwight D. Eisenhower once described leadership as 'the art of getting someone else to do something you want because he wants to do it'. While we're talking about American generals, how about George Patton's belief that 'You don't tell people how to do things, you tell them what you want doing and let them surprise you with the results'. What managers understand is that people are motivated by their own needs, expectations and interests. But great managers know that people also have overarching values that impact on their motivation to do things. Tap into these values and watch the person perform beyond your wildest expectations.

In this section I look at nine theories of motivation. All are useful to the busy manager but some get misused. I've lost count of the number of writers who ignore the fact that many motivational models were based on research obtained from studies of white, male, middle-class employees in the USA in the early 1950s. How applicable something like Maslow's hierarchy of needs might be to an unskilled, largely female workforce in multi-cultural Britain of the twenty-first century is debatable. Therefore, you will have to decide how applicable every theory discussed in this section is in the unique context of your working environment.

The entries discussed emphasise three broad approaches that writers on motivation have taken. These are:

1 Motivation as a force that satisfies people's needs.

2 Theories that examine how the way in which we treat people either motivates or demotivates them.

3 The importance of good communication between managers and staff.

There are similarities as well as some opposing views expressed in the entries. It's up to you to decide whether Maslow's progression theory makes more sense than Alderfer's adaptation theory or whether Vroom's expectancy formula is more powerful than Hackman's job characteristic model. Whatever choices you make the theories will help you to connect with staff at a meaningful level. Read the theories and think about their application and, I promise, you will be able to identify everyone you know or ever will know within one or more of the theories.

One thing that is clear from these entries is that words lead to actions. Therefore, whenever you try to motivate someone think carefully about your message and how you are going to communicate. Think also about how the message will be received, interpreted and acted upon by the recipient. Is that the response you want? Remember, there is often a huge difference between the message you think you sent and the one the person receives.

THEORY 23 MASLOW'S HIERARCHY OF NEEDS THEORY

Use as a general overarching theory that explains people's whole life motivations, many of which will not be satisfied in the world of work.

Abraham Maslow's pyramid represents a hierarchy of needs that must be satisfied in a sequential order from bottom to top. He suggests that failing to satisfy a need at any level will prevent progression to the next level.

Self-fulfilment
Reaching full potential

Esteem
Self-belief and satisfaction
(reputation, respect)

Affiliation
Sense of belonging (affection
and love)

Safety
Freedom from fear
(certainty, stability, organisational)

Biological
Basic survival needs (food, warmth, rest)

The needs can be divided into two categories. Basic needs include biological and safety. Growth needs include affiliation, esteem and self-fulfilment. Maslow argues that people die if their basic needs aren't satisfied and feel inferior and dissatisfied if their affiliation and esteem needs go unfulfilled and if they cannot achieve self-actualisation.

Managers have a responsibility to ensure that an employee's basic needs are met and to create a climate in which employees can develop.

HOW TO USE IT

- Ensure that your team's basic needs are met. These include food, water, warmth, rest and shelter. These equate to a safe working environment free from physical and psychological harm. Heating, lighting and ventilation must meet required standards and you should regularly compare pay and conditions with what your competitors are offering *(see Theory 74)*.

- Once basic needs are met start to work on satisfying some of the higher level needs. Encourage social interaction and team spirit. Some organisations have dress-down Fridays as a means of encouraging less formality and greater interaction.

- People now feel happy and content with life in your organisation. They are well-paid members of a family with a good sense of security and belonging. Build on this by developing opportunities for teamwork *(see Section 4)*.

- Build and enhance your team's self-esteem by designing challenging jobs. Give positive feedback and praise regularly. Delegate responsibility and offer developmental training opportunities. Contentment now becomes excitement as people start to feel valued.

- By now the pyramid is nearly complete but putting the final touch to it may be beyond even the best manager. Most people don't seek to achieve self-actualisation at work. They find that elsewhere. However, you can create the conditions for self-fulfilment by providing challenges for all staff, encouraging creativity and removing any obstacles that might block a person's progress.

QUESTIONS TO ASK

- What are my lifetime ambitions?
- What would count as self-actualisation for me?

THEORY 24   # ALDERFER'S EXISTENCE, RELATEDNESS AND GROWTH (ERG) THEORY

Use when a member of your team has regressed to a lower level of development/motivation and you need to arrest and reverse the decline.

Clayton Alderfer summarised human motivation factors into three categories rather than the five Maslow used. These he called existence, relatedness and growth.

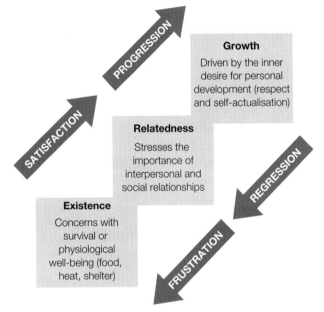

Growth

Driven by the inner desire for personal development (respect and self-actualisation)

Relatedness

Stresses the importance of interpersonal and social relationships

Existence

Concerns with survival or physiological well-being (food, heat, shelter)

PROGRESSION

SATISFACTION

REGRESSION

FRUSTRATION

Source: Adapted from Alderfer, C. P., 'An Empirical Test of a New Theory of Human Need,' *Psychological Review* (1969).

Alderfer maintains that although there is a progression from existence through to growth, all three needs can be operating as motivators simultaneously and it is not uncommon for people to regress to a lower level set of needs.

HOW TO USE IT

■ Compare Alderfer's existence, relatedness and growth needs with Maslow's hierarchy *(see Theory 23)* and you will see that they are almost identical. The difference is that Alderfer suggests that you must address all three sets of needs simultaneously. Focusing on just one at a time will lead to discontent.

■ Frustration at not being able to satisfy all needs may cause staff to regress to one of the lower levels. For example, if you fail to satisfy their need for personal development, they may regress to relatedness needs such as dependence on socialising with workmates or questioning whether pay and conditions are acceptable.

■ If the person starts to regress (disinterest in work or sudden poor attendance or time-keeping) arrest the decline and make sure they don't fall back further. Meet with them and identify as precisely as you can what the problem is. Use Berne's theory *(see Theory 31)* and NLP *(see Theory 84)* to ensure good quality exchanges and try to stabilise the position.

■ Once the problem has been correctly identified, work with the person to agree a plan of action. This will probably require both of you to do something.

■ Ensure that you deliver on what you have promised and monitor on a regular basis that the person is meeting their targets.

■ There will be occasions when you can't stop a person regressing. In such cases try to understand why they have regressed and work with them to address any frustrations they have until they are able to pursue growth again.

QUESTIONS TO ASK

■ Have I reached a plateau in terms of my own personal development and motivation?

■ If so, what am I going to do about it?

THEORY 25 | # McCLELLAND'S ACHIEVEMENT AND ACQUIRED NEEDS THEORY

Use to understand the three overarching needs that people within your team have.

David McClelland proposed the theory that people are motivated by one of three needs: the need for achievement, power or affiliation. He argued that a person's motivation and effectiveness in a specific job function would be influenced by one of these needs.

MCCLELLAND'S ACHIEVEMENT AND ACQUIRED NEEDS THEORY CAN BE SUMMARISED AS:

Achievement (N-Ach): The N-Ach person seeks achievement, attainment of realistic but challenging goals, recognition for a job well done and advancement.

Power (N-Pow): The N-Pow person has a strong desire to motivate or lead others. This can take the form of personalised power which can involve seeking advancement at the expense of others *(see Theory 77).*

Affiliation (N-Affil): The N-Affil person has a need to maintain friendly relationships and interaction with others and seek acceptance from them.

Although the drive to satisfy one of the needs will dominate, individuals will also need to satisfy elements of the other two.

HOW TO USE IT

■ There's no questionnaire to help you here. You'll have to talk to each person individually about what they want from their job and what they think they can contribute to the organisation. Keep the meeting friendly but don't be afraid to ask direct and challenging questions.

■ Based on the information collected identify which of McClelland's three needs dominates each person and develop a strategy for dealing with them.

■ Individuals who have a need for achievement (N-Ach) will thrive when you give them personal responsibility. But they fear failure and may only be prepared to take moderate risks. Give them support and regular feedback but step in if they start to demand too much of other team members who are not as task focused as them *(see Theories 7, 12 and 13)*.

■ Individuals who have a need for power (N-Pow) have a high work ethic and a commitment to the organisation and their job. Which is great. However, many people who seek personalised power don't have the flexibility and people skills required to work well with others. Give them projects to work on alone and keep a watchful eye on them. Step in if their behaviour becomes overly forceful *(see Theories 30, 31 and 83)*.

■ Individuals who have a need for affiliation (N-Affil) are a treasure to work with until their fixation on maintaining good social relationships undermines their ability to do their job. Play to their strengths. Insist that they do their job but allow them time to act as mediator in minor disputes among team members and organise the social activities for the team *(see Theory 32)*.

QUESTIONS TO ASK

■ Which stereotype do I and members of my team fall into?

■ Do I need to change my behaviour or that of my staff?

THEORY 26 # HERZBERG'S MOTIVATION AND HYGIENE THEORY

Use to distinguish between those factors that genuinely motivate staff and those that merely demotivate them when they fall below acceptable levels.

Frederick Herzberg identified two groups of factors. Motivating factors which create satisfaction and hygiene factors which don't provide satisfaction but can be a source of dissatisfaction if they fall below acceptable levels.
The most important factors are:

Hygiene factors	Motivating factors
Pay, company policies, relationship with supervisors, working conditions, feelings associated with lack of status or security	Recognition, achievement, advancement, nature of the work undertaken, responsibility
If these factors fall below a certain level dissatisfaction sets in	If these factors are present staff will feel motivated

Herzberg uses the term KITAs (literally kicks in the ass) when he refers to some of the ineffective strategies used by managers to motivate staff.

THESE ARE:

Negative physical KITAs are literally a kick in the backside and include critical feedback or a right royal rollicking.

Negative psychological KITAs include emotional game playing and physiological manipulation.

Positive KITAs include bonuses, pay increases and benefits. However, he argues that regardless of how generous the positive KITAs are they will not on their own generate positive motivation. But, if they drop below an acceptable level they will cause resentment and de-motivation.

HOW TO USE IT

- Start by recognising that most people are not motivated solely by pay and working conditions.

- Make people's work interesting. Redistribute the more mundane tasks between members of the team and impress on each person the importance of their job to the team's overall performance.

- Give each member of staff the necessary resources and training they need to work effectively. Make them responsible for the quality of their work and give them the autonomy to get on with it. Do this and they will see work as their responsibility and not something they just do for the boss.

- Set challenging but realistic targets which when achieved will give staff a feeling of achievement. Recognise such achievements publicly. Simply saying 'thank you' or 'well done' publicly will do wonders for morale and productivity.

- Provide opportunities for advancement and personal development for all staff. Promote from within whenever possible but remember, providing a new challenge or more interesting work can provide greater motivation than a pay rise or promotion.

- Although factors such as pay and working conditions are not motivational factors, if they fall below a certain level they can be serious de-motivators. Benchmark (see Theory 74) pay and working conditions with similar groups in your organisation and competitors and ensure equivalence.

- Maintain good communications with staff and adopt their good ideas. But make sure that they receive full recognition for their suggestions (see Theory 8).

- Don't be afraid to use negative physical KITAs. By delivering a right rollicking to a member of staff you can often provoke the reaction 'Right, I'll show that b******'. Which is exactly the response you want.

QUESTIONS TO ASK

- Do I assume that what motivates me motivates my staff?
- Do I publicly thank and/or celebrate the success of my staff?

THEORY 27 ADAMS' EQUITY THEORY

Use this to understand how people act when they perceive they are treated differently from another member of staff.

Stacy Adams' equity theory is based on the principle that people are motivated to act in situations where they perceive they have been treated inequitably or unfairly. Adams argues that the more intense the perceived inequity, the higher the tension, and the stronger the motivation to act.

The figure below tracks the perceptions of two different people. A who feels s/he deserves to be treated better than B. And B who feels guilty at not working as hard as A.

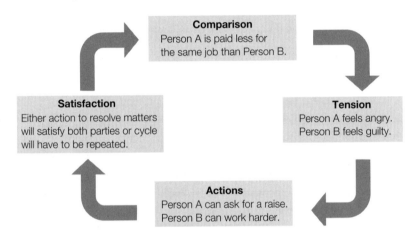

Comparison
Person A is paid less for the same job than Person B.

Tension
Person A feels angry.
Person B feels guilty.

Actions
Person A can ask for a raise.
Person B can work harder.

Satisfaction
Either action to resolve matters will satisfy both parties or cycle will have to be repeated.

A stalemate occurs if neither or both actions take place (e.g. A getting a raise and B working harder simply replaces the focus of the tension).

Employees who perceive inequity will seek to address it by reducing their level of effort, increasing their pay or leaving the organisation.

HOW TO USE IT

- Look for the signs of discontent including sulking, passive or aggressive behaviour, tensions between two or more members of staff, snide remarks during meetings or conversations and general 'dark mutterings'.

- Accept that any sense of inequity stems from the person's perception of how unfairly they have been treated. Such perceptions are seldom based on fact but are driven by emotions.

- Accept that the extent of de-motivation is proportional to the degree of perceived disparity in treatment. You will find that some people feel a huge sense of unfairness at the slightest indication of inequity.

- Recognise that you are dealing with emotions and that they are never logical. Telling someone they are wrong is not always going to work.

- Meet with the person/s concerned. Allow sufficient time for the meeting, it's not going to be done and dusted in ten minutes. Let each person tell their story and blow off steam without interruption. This by itself will lower the temperature.

- Many people have misconceptions about what is equitable. Some have delusions of adequacy and an inflated view of their importance to the organisation. If they are not as indispensable as they think you need to tell them. They won't like it but you must confront them with the reality of the situation. Not what they think it is *(see Theory 83)*.

- If you discover that inequality exists, deal with it. And while you are at it, check if your dispute is just a symptom of a wider problem in the organisation.

QUESTIONS TO ASK

- What is the precise problem I am facing?
- Is it a problem of recognition masquerading as an issue about pay or conditions?

THEORY 28 # VROOM'S EXPECTANCY THEORY

Use this to understand why people react to certain work-based requests or promises as they do.

Victor Vroom suggested that an individual will behave in a certain way based upon the belief (expectation) that a specific act will be followed by a desired reward (valence) once the act has been completed (instrumentality).

He expressed his expectancy theory of motivation in terms of a mathematical formula: Motivation = Valence × Expectancy × Instrumentality. If any one of the three factors is nil, the overall score will be zero, and there will be nil motivation.

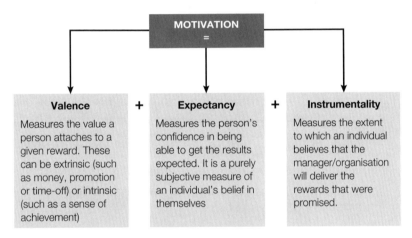

The model assumes that it is possible for the manager to score these three factors when in reality they are subjective and incredibly difficult to assess in ourselves let alone in another person.

HOW TO USE IT

- Don't dismiss Vroom's theory just because people don't consciously allocate scores to concepts like valence, expectancy and instrumentality, and if they did how the hell could you as a manager guess what they were? People may not use the jargon or consciously identify and weigh up the factors in the terms that Vroom describes but they do think in terms of: What do I want? How likely is it that I can get it? Will the organisation deliver on its promises?

- So forget about the scores. Instead, find out what your employees want from their job and provide work that is economically beneficial and/or intrinsically motivating for them. This will have the effect of creating rewards that they really want *(see Theory 26)*.

- If expectancy is all about effort and results, make sure that you create an environment where effort is both encouraged and rewarded and employees have access to the resources, equipment and materials they need to get results.

- Strengthen the instrumentality link in the chain by keeping your promises and distancing yourself from those that don't.

- It's no good delivering on two out of the three factors because, as shown by Vroom, failure to deliver on any one results in nil motivation.

QUESTIONS TO ASK

- Which factor (if any) would I and my staff give a score of zero to – valence, expectancy or instrumentality?

- Even if there are no zero scores what can I do to show staff that good work is recognised and rewarded?

THEORY 29 **THE HACKMAN AND OLDHAM JOB CHARACTERISTIC MODEL**

Use to remind you that autonomy and feedback are powerful motivating factors, cost nothing to provide and should be built into the design of every job/task.

Richard Hackman and Greg Oldham's theory is based on the principle that employees derive motivation from completing a task.

They suggest that high levels of motivation occur as a result of three critical psychological states.

THESE ARE:

Meaningfulness: The employee must consider the task to be meaningful.

Responsibility: The employee must have sufficient discretion to plan and carry out the task as they see fit.

Feedback: The employee must be aware of how effective they have been.

Hackman and Oldham claim that satisfaction in each of these states can be derived as a result of effective task design.

HOW TO USE IT

- Recognise that some jobs *are* boring and monotonous! Then do something to relieve the boredom and provide meaning.

- As far as possible ensure that an employee can work on a task from start to finish and see a visible end product. Show them the importance of their work and how their efforts affect the work of other people in the organisation and the end customer *(see Theory 1)*. During the Second World War the women who packed parachutes regularly met with flight crews. This significantly reduced the number of chutes that failed to open!

- Encourage staff to use a variety of skills and abilities to complete the task. Give them the freedom to choose their own working methods and control the resources they need to complete the task.

- Provide feedback to each person on a regular basis and give them clear and direct information about how well they performed at critical stages throughout the task.

- Use work rotation within the team to avoid staleness. Do this and staff will gain a greater understanding of the contribution that each member of the team makes to the final outcome.

- If job rotation doesn't work challenge individuals to come up with a design for their job that will make it more interesting. If they do come up with an efficient new design let them try it out. If the experiment fails, so what? At least you listened to the member of staff *(see Theory 4)*.

QUESTIONS TO ASK

- How much autonomy and variety do I offer staff?
- How much feedback do I give staff?

THEORY 30 **ERNST'S OK CORRAL MODEL**

Use to understand how your feelings about yourself and others affect your work.

Franklyn Ernst suggested that the way we regard ourselves and those we interact with influences our attitudes and emotional states and hence our behaviour. He represented this theory as a 2×2 matrix with the one axis depicting the level of value of others (I'm okay with you) and the other one's own self-value (I'm okay with me).

THE CHARACTERISTICS OF THE FOUR QUADRANTS ARE:

I'm okay with me – I'm not okay with you: This situation is characterised by anger and you trying to coerce the other person and/or get one over on them.

I'm not okay with me – I'm okay with you: This is characterised by your feelings of lack of worth and fear and a willingness to allow the other person to get what they want.

I'm okay with me – I'm okay with you: This is the happy harmonious situation, characterised by constructive and cooperative relationships.

I'm not OK with me – I'm not OK with you: This is a horrible place to be and you need to get out of it before you descend into depression and self-loathing.

Ernst's theory can be used to challenge people's old belief systems and replace them with more constructive thoughts about how they feel about themselves and others.

HOW TO USE IT

- Identify where you are on the model. Be honest.
- Identify your feelings towards the other person and locate your opinion on the grid.
- Recognise that where you are on the model and how you feel about yourself and the other person can change from day to day.
- If you're not OK with the person you need to change your outlook. Identify why you feel as you do. Often this will have nothing to do with work issues. You may be jealous of them, fear them or think they are wasting their talent. You have to park such feelings and accept the person for what they are: an imperfect human being.
- Much more problematic is if you're not OK with yourself. You too are an imperfect human being – so give yourself a break and stop setting unachievable standards for yourself.
- No one knows if people are born with a lack of self-belief or if it's drained out of them by life. What is clear is that self-fulfilling prophecies play a role in destroying self-belief. Keep telling someone 'you're stupid' and guess what? Keep telling yourself 'I'm stupid' and the implications are even clearer. Every time you catch yourself thinking like that, challenge the thought.
- Replace negative thinking with positive self-talk. Rehearse in your mind social and work-related scenarios where you come out on top and replace the word 'can't' with 'can' or 'why not' *(see Theories 11 and 84).*
- As your sense of self-value increases, so will the value you attach to other people.

QUESTIONS TO ASK

- Who was it that told me I'm no good? My parents, a teacher or my boss?
- What power do they have over me today? Probably none. So why am I affected by what they said?

THEORY 31   # BERNE'S THEORY OF TRANSACTIONAL ANALYSIS (CROWN AS KING)

Use this to become a more effective communicator.

Transactional analysis theory describes the state of mind that a person is in when they give or receive a message. The way managers communicate with staff has a significant effect on how staff receive, interpret and act upon the broadcast message. Berne identified five patterns of behaviour, or ego states, that people use when communicating.

THE CHARACTERISTICS OF EACH EGO STATE ARE:

The critical parent state: The person is overbearing and tells people what to do.

The nurturing parent state: The person expresses concern for people's feelings but likes to tell people what to do in the guise of offering advice.

The free child state: The person expresses their emotions without constraint.

The adaptive child state: The person lacks confidence and is anxious to please.

The adult ego state: The person acts with maturity and assesses the situation in a calm and rational manner.

Although behaving in the adult ego state is generally the most effective approach, Berne suggests that there are times when managers may need to adopt the parent or even the child ego state in order to motivate employees.

HOW TO USE IT

■ Recognise that you have the ability to adopt any ego state.

■ To use transactional analysis identify which ego state your staff are in and adopt the ego state that is most effective in dealing with them.

■ If you are both in a parent ego state then the likelihood is that there will be friction as you both try to impose your own rules on the other.

■ If you are both in a child ego state you might have a bit of fun but nothing will get done because you will be too busy sucking your thumbs and throwing your teddies out of the crib.

■ If you are in the parent ego state and the other person is in the child ego state or vice versa then this will produce an outcome satisfactory to at least one side, but this may be short-lived.

■ The ideal state to aim for is when you are both in the adult ego state.

■ To move from either the parent or child ego states ask questions such as: What can we do about this? How I can I support you to get this done? How can we sort this? How would you suggest we move forward? If you follow this simple process it will improve your ability to manage and motivate your staff significantly. Give it a try.

QUESTIONS TO ASK

■ Which is my normal state? Is it a productive state? If not, how can I change it?

■ What causes me to shift states? Is it words, actions or events?

A FINAL WORD ON MOTIVATION THEORIES

WHY BERNE'S THEORY WAS CROWNED KING

Berne's theory suggests that communication involves a set of hidden transactions. It was considered too radical at the time of its publication in the 1960s and has only really been used by managers since the 1990s.

I chose this theory because it emphasises that how we talk to people has a greater impact on their levels of motivation than such things as pay and conditions. If management is about relationships then it's essential that you communicate in a respectful and adult manner with your staff and guide them to the position where they too communicate with you in the same vein.

Of course, you and your staff will disagree on a range of issues but don't make matters worse by adopting the wrong ego state.

According to Maslow, progression towards self-fulfilment depends on a stable foundation where lower level needs must be satisfied before higher needs can be addressed. As you get to know people better, you will identify what they want from work. However, it's just plain daft to assume that everyone will find self-actualisation in work. Most will be more than happy to draw their salary and find fulfilment away from the workplace in sport, dancing, family life, playing chess or supporting local charities. This does not mean that work can't satisfy many of their needs. Everyone wants to feel that their work is meaningful, that they do a good job, have the respect of colleagues and are part of a team. It's these wants that you need to concentrate on. Increased pay and improved working conditions on their own will not motivate staff. However, if such hygiene factors fall below acceptable standards discontent and demotivation will quickly spread throughout the team.

Whatever level of satisfaction people wish to achieve at work, never under-estimate the importance of allowing autonomy and giving feedback as motivational tools. Even the most mundane job can be rewarding if the person doing it can exercise a reasonable level of control over how they undertake their work. Combine this with regular feedback and many people will be perfectly happy to get on with their work and monitor their own performance.

In order to maintain a happy workforce be on the lookout for any signs that a member of staff harbours resentment about how they are treated. If you see signs of sulking, uncooperativeness or poor work, find out what's causing the feeling of unfairness and take immediate action. If you are slow in reacting, the problem will fester, grow and infect others.

From time to time people may regress from where they are currently at to a lower level of engagement with work. They may do this because of changes in their life and/or new priorities or because of events at work. Allow people to regress temporarily if they need to but don't let them dwell there indefinitely. Work with them to resolve or come to terms with any problems that are impacting on their level of motivation and encourage them to move on as quickly as possible. This is important because as manager you need all employees to contribute fully to the team's objectives.

To help any member of staff get back on track you have to use the right blend of encouragement, command, control and support. That's where Berne's theory comes into its own. If you identify what ego state they are in you can use the What? Why? When? How? questions to guide them to the adult–adult ego state where issues can be discussed and resolved in an atmosphere of mutual respect.

Whichever approach you take with staff remember that motivation is all about matching rewards to effort and achievement. To maintain a motivated staff you have to deliver on your promises. Break these and any chance you have of motivating staff will disappear quicker than a morning frost in the Sahara Desert.

Finally, don't forget to motivate yourself. Use positive self-talk and visualisation to improve your own self-confidence/belief and celebrate your own success in whatever way you find most rewarding.

SECTION 4

HOW TO BUILD AND MANAGE TEAMS

INTRODUCTION

Before we get into talking about teams I want to make one thing clear. Building and managing teams is difficult and even the best managers can get it wrong sometimes.

In the 1966 World Cup Final Alf Ramsey took the unpopular decision to leave out his star striker for the final against West Germany. Instead he picked Geoff Hurst whose style better suited his team plan. Geoff scored the only ever hat-trick in a World Cup Final and England became World Champions. But four years later, in Mexico, Sir Alf made the catastrophic decision to substitute Bobby Charlton when England were two up against West Germany in the quarter final and ended up losing 3–2. If it can happen to Alf Ramsey at the height of his career it can happen to you. If it does, don't be too hard on yourself. Learn from your mistakes and move on. After all, it's not as if someone will still be talking about your cock-up 40-odd years from now.

In order for people to find a reason to work as a member of a team, they need a common purpose and a sense of identity. Put a group of people in a lift together and they think and act as individuals. Create a crisis situation such as a breakdown or fire in the lift shaft and the need for survival becomes the common purpose. Instinctively each person assumes a role that they think will help the group survive, for example tactician, comforter, problem solver etc.

In this part, I examine the roles that people play within teams and the factors that may affect their capacity to perform effectively. The role that managers play in promoting effective team-working is also considered.

The British management guru Charles Handy tells a good story of how, when addressing a group of undergraduates, he once described ineffective teams as being like a rowing crew with eight people going backwards without talking to one another, being guided by someone who is too small to see where they were going. He admitted that he got a bit of flak from a rower in the audience who argued that, on the contrary, they were a good example of the perfect team; as they would not have the confidence to pull on the oar so strongly without talking or seeing if they didn't have complete trust in each other and in the person steering the boat. I like Handy, but in this instance I think the rowers beat him by a canvas.

I'll leave it to the American car magnate Henry Ford to sum up what this section is all about. He described team formation as 'Coming together is a beginning; keeping together is a process; working together is success.'

THEORY 32   # BELBIN'S TEAM ROLES

Use as a checklist, every time you form a new team, to confirm that you have the right mix of people for the job.

For any team to be successful, Meredith Belbin argues that the following roles must be undertaken by nominated members of the team:

Source: Team roles and descriptions adapted courtesy of Belbin Associates.

- **Chair/Co-ordinator** sets the agenda, is calm and confident and responsible for getting the balance of the team right.
- **Shaper** aims to influence the team's decisions; is extrovert and willing to be unpopular if the job requires it.
- **Plant/innovator** generates ideas and develops innovative ways to solve problems.
- **Monitor/evaluator** is analytical, dispassionate and objective, but may upset team mates with criticisms.
- **Implementer** works hard to turn ideas into action; may annoy team mates because of their reluctance to compromise.
- **Resource investigators** are often crafty and personable; they find the resources required and suss out what the opposition is up to.
- **Teamworker** is sociable and conscientious; brings the team together and helps sort out any of the team's inter-personal and professional issues.

- **Completer/finisher** is determined and committed but can be seen as too keen to get the job done at any cost.
- **Specialist** provides technical expertise in key areas; may annoy others because they focus too narrowly on their specialist area.

HOW TO USE IT

- Start with the end in mind *(see Theory 9)* and identify the team's aims and objectives, the resources available and the deadlines you must meet.
- Identify who supports/opposes the project *(see Theory 55)*. This information is vital. During any project problems will arise and you need to know who you can trust.
- Make sure that the recruits to your team can cover all of the functions listed on the facing page – even if that means some people covering two or more functions.
- Use a combination of personal interviews and Belbin's Team Roles Questionnaire (available online) to identify each person's role/s.
- Brief each person on what you expect of them. Then monitor progress, identify problems and implement remedies. If you're not the problem (and managers often are) consider the following:
  - A lack of clarity about the team's objectives. What's your Shaper doing?
  - Underperformance by the team. How good is your Completer?
  - An inability to overcome problems. What's your Plant doing?
  - Poor analysis of problems. Does your Monitor need a wake-up call?
  - Difficulties in turning ideas into practical solutions. What's your Implementer up to?
  - Lack of resources. Do you need to replace your Resource Investigator with someone who can duck and dive.
  - A lack of harmony and commitment to the team's objectives. Has the Teamworker upset the team?
  - An inability to finish tasks. Has your Completer become bored with the project?
  - Lack of specialist knowledge. Does your Specialist have the right expertise for the project?

Once you have identified the problem deal with it decisively.

QUESTIONS TO ASK

- Do I have the right mix of people in the team?
- How will I monitor progress? What are my milestones?

THEORY 33 MACCOBY'S GAMESMAN THEORY

Use to identify the type of leader your team needs.

Michael Maccoby concentrated on the role and responsibilities of the team manager. He identified four character types that can be found acting as team manager:

- **Craftsman:** Leads by issuing commands and expects staff to follow orders. Individualistic, they can be inventive, self-contained, resolute and sincere but also obstinate and suspicious.

- **Jungle fighter:** Tough, bold and competitive. They thrive on power and the desire to win and will fight to protect the team. But they can also be ego-driven, paternalistic and authoritarian and upset team members with their aggressive attitude.

- **Company man:** A true team player who is loyal, hard-working and eager to please. They thrive on creating an atmosphere of discipline and order but are too conservative to lead a team where innovative thinking or risk taking is required.

- **Gamesman:** A risk taker who is fascinated by new techniques and ideas and loves problem solving. They thrive on competition and generate enthusiasm within the team. But they can be detached, dispassionate and fail to inspire loyalty.

HOW TO USE IT

- Identify which stereotype you are. Be realistic when you make this call. Better still, ask others what characteristics you display. Don't use the terminology that Maccoby uses – that might scare people. Depending on the relationship you have with team members you can be blunt or subtle with your questioning. The important thing is to find out how you are perceived.

- Once you know what staff think of you take action to emphasise the positive aspects of your character and minimise the negative. Consider importing some of the virtues of the other characters. Of course some characteristics could be ingrained and you may find it difficult to change *(see Theory 11)*. For example, a Company Man might struggle to lead a team where blue sky, innovative thinking is required. In this instance, delegate the role of leading on innovation to one of the other members of the team *(see Theory 32)*.

- Recognise that different types of team leaders are required at different stages of the team's evolution. Craftsmen are essential in the beginning, making tools and weapons for protection. Jungle Fighters use the tools to conquer the environment and make it safe. Once the environment has been tamed, Company Men move in and start the socialisation process. As people become a cohesive unit Gamesmen move in and drive the survivors to higher levels of performance.

QUESTIONS TO ASK

- At what stage of development is the organisation/team?

- What type of leader does the team require? Can I provide that type of leadership? If not, whose help on the team can I enlist?

THEORY 34 LIKERT'S THEORY OF TEAM MANAGEMENT STYLES

Use this to understand the role, responsibilities and relationships that you have with your team.

Rensis Likert identified four styles to describe the role, responsibilities and relationships that managers have with their team. The four styles run from autocratic despot to a first-among-equals approach to management and have clear links with style leadership *(see Theories 12 and 13)*.

LIKERT'S MANAGEMENT STYLES:

Exploitive-autocratic: The manager has little or no trust in team members and therefore decisions are imposed with minimal consultation. Communication is top down.

Benevolent-authoritative: The manager is condescending towards the team therefore team members are very reluctant to offer ideas or suggestions. Communication upwards is censored.

Consultative: The manager has significant but not complete confidence in the team. Although there is discussion on key issues there is little doubt as to who has the final say. Communication is mostly top-down but there are signs of cautious bottom-up streams of communication.

Participative: The manager encourages free and open communication throughout the team. New ideas are welcomed. Rewards and punishments are not necessary as the team assumes full responsibility for getting things done. Everyone has absolute confidence in everyone else.

Likert's categories clearly run from a highly task-oriented team management style to a highly people-oriented management style.

HOW TO USE IT

- Identify which team management style you prefer. You could use Blake and Mouton's Questionnaire to do this *(see Theory 13)*.

- As circumstances change, analyse the situation and identify which management approach will be most effective in the new situation.

- Be prepared to vary your style of management depending on circumstances. If you need something done quickly and to a precise standard then an autocratic and authoritarian approach may be required. Once the panic is over you can focus more on the democratic, participative approach. It's all about balancing the needs of the individual, task and organisation *(see Theory 14)* and recognising that these are constantly changing.

- Adopting the correct approach when under pressure is difficult to do. So rehearse different scenarios in your mind before you are faced by them in practice. Know how you will react, why you will react in that way, the impact that the change will have on your team and how you are going to deal with any fallout *(see Theory 67)*.

QUESTIONS TO ASK

- What is my default style of management?
- Which style of management does my team respond to best?

THEORY 35 # DREXLER/SIBBET TEAM PERFORMANCE MODEL®

Use this to identify the stages that a project team will go through and the key questions you need to ask at each stage.

The model was developed by Allan Drexler, David Sibbet and Russ Forrester. It consists of a seven-stage questioning process which is depicted as a bouncing ball.

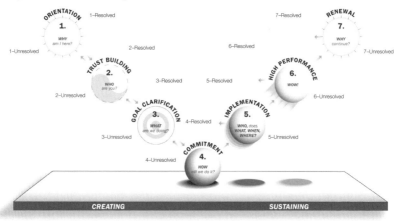

Source: 12.3 TPModel © 1990–2011 Alan Drexler and David Sibbet.

Questions to ask at each stage of the process:

1 **Orientation:** What's the purpose of the team and who's going to be in it?

2 **Trust building:** How can I develop mutual respect, frankness and reliability among the team members?

3 **Goal clarification:** What are we seeking to achieve? How will I ensure that the team has a shared vision and clear unambiguous targets?

4 **Commitment:** How are we going to achieve our target? Do we have the right people and resources to be successful?

5 **Implementation:** Who does what, when and where?

6 **High performance:** How can we ensure that everyone is aligned behind the same objective, are well disciplined and know what they have to do?

7 **Renewal:** When and how will we know that our work is done?

In the stages towards the top of the diagram (the beginning and end), teams often feel a sense of freedom where there are opportunities for limitless potential and possibility. As a team moves through the middle stages there are more constraints with goals being set and decisions made about what can and can't be included in the process.

HOW TO USE IT

- Start by asking yourself and the team 'Why are we here?' Resolve that and you'll get a sense of purpose, team identity and buy-in. Fail to resolve it and you will be faced with confusion, uncertainty and fear.

- Use the questions posed in the theory at each stage of the process to help you progress to the next stage.

- Build inter-team trust by getting members to share details of their work experiences, expectations, agendas and skills. It's during this phase that people test each other out.

- Build on the trust created by making sure that team members are clear about their individual roles and responsibilities and those of their colleagues.

- Produce a detailed implementation plan which identifies who is responsible for each stage of the process *(see Theories 39, 49 and 86)*.

- Use team meetings to clarify the project's aims and monitor progress. Encourage the team to discuss their work and identify different ways of doing things. Expect some disagreement during this stage and only move on when consensus has been reached.

- If you want your team to commit to the project and work cooperatively you must be a good role model – a case of do as I do.

- Don't be afraid to go back to previous stages if you need to. Remember the concept of the model as a bouncing ball and on occasions the ball can run out of steam or not bounce as expected.

- Once the task has been completed celebrate the team's success and discuss areas for improvement and what can be done differently next time.

QUESTIONS TO ASK

- Am I clear about the aims of the project?
- Have I communicated that vision clearly to the team?

THEORY 36 # HOMANS' THEORY OF GROUP FORMATION

Use to identify the external factors which can disrupt/destroy your project.

George Homans argues that the interaction between the group and the environment in which it operates shapes both the behaviour of the group and the final outcome.

THE FIVE FACTORS IDENTIFIED ARE:

Physical restraints that are imposed on the team which affect the performance of the task.

Cultural–personal beliefs and values that make up the shared understanding of the group.

Technological facilities and resources that are available to the team to help them achieve their task.

Organisation's policies and procedures that govern working practices and personal development of team members.

Socio-economic factors which flow from the impact that the wider political, economic, social and technological developments have on the team.

Homan argues that, influenced by the environment, the group goes through a series of behavioural stages. In the beginning they act in a manner expected by the group leader (required or given behaviours) followed by a stage of doing things over and above what is expected (emergent behaviours) resulting ultimately in increased productivity and personal development.

HOW TO USE IT

■ Recognise that you and your team do not operate in isolation. You are both affected by your organisation's culture *(see Section 5)* and wider societal influences.

■ Use SWOT *(see Theory 65)* and PEST/PESTLE *(see Theory 66)* tools to identify the variables that might impact on your project and in conjunction with the team decide how you will deal with all eventualities identified.

■ Remove any physical restraints imposed on your team as this will affect its performance. If accommodation is cramped, over-crowded and separated geographically from the site of the action your team will naturally assume that the organisation thinks that their work is unimportant *(see Theories 23 and 26)*.

■ Instil in the team a common set of values and beliefs about how the team will operate, deal with the task in hand and recognise what a successful outcome will look like.

■ Train every member of your team to maximise the use of the tools available to them. Too often individuals are unaware of what resources are available or how to fully exploit them.

■ Teams working outside the normal organisation structure can be hamstrung by the bureaucracy that governs everyday organisational life. Agree with management to what extent you can opt out of normal controls.

QUESTIONS TO ASK

■ Am I too focused on what is going on within the organisation?

■ Do I need to discuss the wider implications of the project with someone outside the team?

THEORY 37

TUCKMAN'S GROUP DEVELOPMENT SEQUENCE MODEL (CROWN AS KING)

Use this to identify the stages of development that your team pass through and amend your management style accordingly.

Bruce Tuckman first presented his *Forming*, *Storming*, *Norming*, *Performing* (FSNP) model in 1965 and, with Mary Jensen, added a fifth stage (*Adjourning*) in 1977. The model describes the phases which teams go through from initial formation to completion of the task.

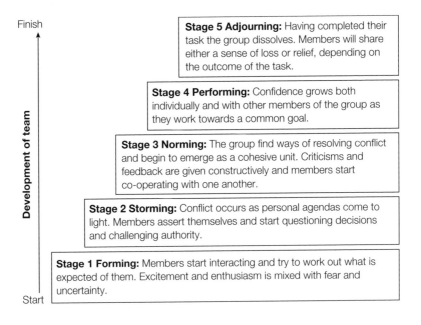

Finish

Stage 5 Adjourning: Having completed their task the group dissolves. Members will share either a sense of loss or relief, depending on the outcome of the task.

Stage 4 Performing: Confidence grows both individually and with other members of the group as they work towards a common goal.

Stage 3 Norming: The group find ways of resolving conflict and begin to emerge as a cohesive unit. Criticisms and feedback are given constructively and members start co-operating with one another.

Stage 2 Storming: Conflict occurs as personal agendas come to light. Members assert themselves and start questioning decisions and challenging authority.

Stage 1 Forming: Members start interacting and try to work out what is expected of them. Excitement and enthusiasm is mixed with fear and uncertainty.

Development of team

Start

HOW TO USE IT

■ Provide guidance from the moment the team starts to form. Make clear the team's purpose, aims and objectives and what contribution you expect from each person. Negotiate and agree working ground rules and listen to any concerns that members have and address them.

■ During the storming phase be prepared to deal with any challenges to your authority or inter-team squabbles. How you deal with these will set the tone for the behaviours you can expect people to exhibit throughout the operational life of the team. Acting passively or aggressively may not be in the team's best interest. Go for a win/win solution *(see Theory 9)* whenever possible.

■ As the team matures and enters the norming phase your role changes to one of supporter. By this stage the team will have developed its own ways of dealing with conflict and created enough trust between team members to accept constructive criticism without coming to blows. So sit back and let the team resolve its own problems.

■ Once the group start performing as a cohesive team don't be afraid to adopt a watching brief. Let the team get on with it. If you've trained them right they will only approach you if they need help.

■ Once the task is complete, celebrate the team's success and acknowledge everyone's contribution.

QUESTIONS TO ASK

■ Do I have the self-discipline to increasingly take a back seat as the team matures?

■ How will I know if I am are stifling the team's growth? What signs will I look for?

THEORY 38 # WHEELAN'S INTEGRATED MODEL OF GROUP DEVELOPMENT

Use this, to deepen your understanding of the developmental stages that groups go through.

Susan Wheelan built on Tuckman's model *(see Theory 37)* and suggested that groups achieve maturity simply through the process of working together. She claims that there is a significant relationship between the length of time that a group has been together and their behavioural patterns. She describes these relationships using a four-stage model based on a life-growth cycle.

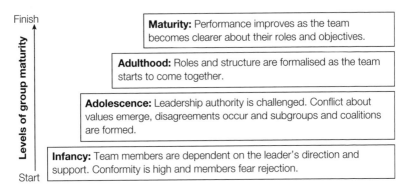

Maturity: Performance improves as the team becomes clearer about their roles and objectives.

Adulthood: Roles and structure are formalised as the team starts to come together.

Adolescence: Leadership authority is challenged. Conflict about values emerge, disagreements occur and subgroups and coalitions are formed.

Infancy: Team members are dependent on the leader's direction and support. Conformity is high and members fear rejection.

To accompany the model Wheelan developed a Group Development Observation System (GDOS) which assesses each member's perception of what stage they think the team is at. Using this information managers can change their management style to match the teams developmental stage and meet its needs.

HOW TO USE IT

▪ Use the Group Development Observation System (GDOS) (available online) to assess each member's perception of what stage they think the team is at.

▪ In phase one (infancy) look out for team members who display the characteristics shown in infancy such as dependency, immaturity and a need to be wanted. Invest time and effort with these people. Explain what you want, answer questions, provide support and model the behaviour you expect from them.

▪ In phase two (adolescence) you can expect conflicts about values, challenges to your authority, disagreements and fights to break out. Remain calm and remember that it's not personal *(see Theories 31 and 84)*. Provide both opportunities and time for staff to talk to you and each other. Use these conversations to emphasise the shared values that you expect the team to exhibit.

▪ In phase three back off as the team enters young adulthood. If you want the team to reach full maturity, you must resist becoming too involved with the team's decision making. Act as a facilitator not a director and let the team sort out its own mistakes.

▪ Phase four (maturity) is where your team have the confidence and belief to tackle even the most challenging tasks alone. Allow them space, don't interfere, but keep a familial eye on them and celebrate their achievements. They may have cut the apron strings but (hopefully) they will still respect you and value your advice, praise and appreciation.

QUESTIONS TO ASK

▪ Do I have the ability to support my team members through each phase?

▪ Is there someone outside the team who I can talk to in confidence to help me with this?

THEORY 39 · LOCKE'S GOAL SETTING THEORY

Use when you want to motivate, monitor and control staff by using targets.

Edwin Locke claimed that there was a relationship between how difficult and specific a goal was and how well a team performed.

The five principles that underpin successful goal setting:

- **Clarity:** When a goal is clear and specific, there is less misunderstanding within the team about who is expected to do what, to what standard and within what timeframe.
- **Challenge:** Teams are motivated by challenge and achievement. A 'good' goal is one which is difficult but do-able and which team members believe will give them great satisfaction when achieved.
- **Commitment:** Teams are more likely to 'buy into' a goal if they feel they were part of creating the goal.
- **Feedback:** Teams react positively to action by the leader that clarifies expectations, adjusts goals and acknowledges achievement.
- **Task complexity:** Teams may get excited by working on challenging tasks but they may also get overwhelmed if the task is too complex.

Locke asserts that the underlying purpose of goal setting is to facilitate success. If managers fail to make targets clear and specific they will frustrate and inhibit staff from achieving their objectives.

HOW TO USE IT

■ Recognise that if your team isn't operating as effectively as it should the problem may lie with you. Did you set specific, measurable, achievable, realistic and time-limited goals (SMART targets – *see Theory 88)*? If not, redraw them. Ensure that each goal is both challenging and realistic. Aim too high and you'll de-motivate your team. Aim too low and the team will become bored and disinterested.

■ Once you have set SMART targets ask staff to set their own individual targets. Have them use the SMART approach and make sure that their targets are compatible with the team's goals. By doing this, you keep everyone motivated and committed to an integrated set of personal and team goals.

■ Provide regular feedback to both individuals and the team but don't go overboard. You don't need daily team meetings or meetings to agree agendas for meetings etc. Instead, provide feedback as and when you come into daily contact with people and hold short, snappy meetings to discuss and record progress.

■ For complex tasks take special care to ensure that you don't overwhelm the team. Those team members who are used to working on complex tasks may be straining to strut their stuff. But less experienced staff may feel under severe pressure to perform. Keep an eye on them and talk to them regularly *(see Theory 16)*.

QUESTIONS TO ASK

■ Have I set SMART targets for the team and each person in it?

■ Do my meetings help the team achieve its targets or slow it down?

A FINAL WORD ON TEAM THEORIES

WHY TUCKMAN WAS CROWNED KING

This was a real toughie. The choice lay between Belbin and Tuckman with Wheelan a very close third. I've used Belbin extensively in the past but opted for Tuckman because he emphasises the actions you need to take to forge a group of individuals into a great team. His process is simple but brilliant. You need to get them:

- together;
- talking;
- thinking along the same lines;
- resolving conflicts; and
- taking responsibility for their own work/performance

while you stand back, act as facilitator and watch them grow (Wheelan's perspective on this as a life-growth cycle is fascinating).

When choosing team members it's not only essential to have people with the skills Belbin identified but also people who can complement your strengths and compensate for your weaknesses. For example, it's perfectly possible to lead a team that has to deliver a major new computer system within six months yet have little knowledge of computing, provided you surround yourself with great people who know their stuff and who you trust. I know, because I did it thanks to a great team.

Once you have your team, spend time clarifying your aims and objectives. Whatever your aim is you can only 'build it' if you have a clear picture of what 'it' will look like when complete. Don't go off half-cocked. Be certain about where you want to go before you take a single step. Only then should you brief each person individually on their roles and responsibilities. Then brief the entire team on who is responsible for what. This will clarify roles and responsibilities, eliminate confusion and enable the team to hold its own members to account (see Theory 4).

Set SMART targets that will motivate both individuals and the team. Make a point of recognising people's contribution to the project and celebrating even small successes.

One of the first tasks that you and the team need to perform is to evaluate the environment in which you will be operating. You can be the world's greatest manager but if the environment you are operating in is poisonous you stand little chance of success. Use scanning tools (see

Theories 36, 65 and 66) to examine the internal and external factors that might affect the project. Be aware that while external factors can damage you it's the internal factors that are most likely to kill your team.

As the team starts to work and develop its own personality be aware that you may need to change your management style. Part of any maturation process involves learning to deal with your own problems. At some stage you must give the group the freedom to deal with its own conflicts. You may be tempted to intervene but if you do you'll stunt team growth.

The way team building is often portrayed is that it's a linear process. Even this conclusion gives that impression. The truth is, if things start to go wrong you may have to take more than one step back in order to resolve a problem before you can move on.

Great teams can do great things. One of the most remarkable examples of team building and subsequent success in recent years was England's victory in the 2003 Rugby World Cup. The head coach, Clive Woodward, attributed England's success not just to an outstanding group of players, but to having the most intensive preparation of any international team and a powerful team spirit both on and off the pitch. He paid particular tribute to the roles filled with precision and passion by the many players and backroom staff that made up the team. In summary, he was reiterating that great military saying 'Planning Prevents P*** Poor Performance'.

SECTION 5

HOW TO ANALYSE ORGANISATIONAL CULTURE

INTRODUCTION

The aim of this section is to help you identify the culture that exists in your organisation. The entries give advice on how to use the theories with your staff but their main purpose is to help you identify and understand the culture you work in. This is vital. If you are at odds with your organisation's culture you will find it a very uncomfortable environment to work in. I once worked for a chief executive who made the Emperor Caligula's decision-making processes seem well balanced and logical. It was a power culture *(see Theory 40)* and as he held all the power he did whatever took his fancy. I couldn't cope with such an arbitrary approach to management and as I couldn't change it, I left.

If your organisation's culture is just mildly irksome you may decide to stay. In which case, you may need to adjust your management style to suit the prevailing culture. If you don't, you'll be like the salmon swimming upstream – brave but likely to get caught out by a bloody big bear or some guy with a rod and line.

But what is organisational culture? I once asked a group of staff from a major car manufacturer that very question. Their answers ranged from 'religious beliefs' through to 'the thing that grows in the bottom of your cup if you don't wash it on a Friday night'.

I had been looking for a response along the lines of the principles, ideologies, policies and practices shared by all within an organisation. Diplomatically, I acknowledged each contribution with comments such as 'values and beliefs certainly impact on culture' and 'just like the blobby bits in your unwashed cup, culture is an organic process in which the end product can have both a harmful or healing effect'. (Personally I've never bought the idea that Alexander Fleming discovered penicillin on a piece of old bread.)

The range of responses demonstrates the complexity of the subject. There are many approaches to culture and even more definitions. Kroeber and Kluckhohn, in their review of organisational culture in the 1950s, reported 156 different definitions. And that was before the management gurus of the 1960s–90s got started. Unfortunately, there is still no consensus as to exactly what is meant by organisational culture. Don't be alarmed by this lack of consensus as just searching for a common definition helps us understand the idea of organisational culture better.

The entries in this section range from the pragmatic to the wildly metaphorical. What they have in common is that they give you different and interesting ways to analyse and think about your organisation's culture. What is it? How was it established? How is it maintained? What influence does it exert over the people in the organisation?

Although organisational cultures do vary widely from one institution to the next, similarities also exist. Most organisational cultures can be categorised as something that an organisation *is* (the image people have of how the organisation goes about its business) or something that an organisation *has* (its fundamental values and beliefs).

Read the following and use those ideas that appeal to you and which you can see yourself using in the workplace. All I ask is that you don't rely on just one or two theories. Organisational culture is multi-faceted and you need to look at it from several angles if you hope to get a clear picture of the environment you are operating in.

HANDY'S MODEL OF ORGANISATIONAL CULTURE (CROWN AS KING)

Use Handy's organisational culture questionnaire when you want to get a quick overview of your culture and how you feel about it.

Charles Handy suggests that all organisational cultures are comprised of four different sub-cultures. It is the precise mix/influence of these sub-cultures that produce the organisation's unique culture. The sub-cultures are:

Club (or power)	Role (or bureaucratic)
A spider's web portrays this culture. The spider is all-powerful and if they move the web shakes and everyone jumps. In club cultures power resides with one person or a small elite.	A Greek temple describes this culture. Each pillar of the temple represents a key function/department. The organisation's structure is hierarchical and staff are expected to work to their job description and follow laid-down rules and procedures.
Task (or team)	**Existential (or individual)**
A net represents this culture. Teamwork is extensively used to resolve problems. On completion of the task the team is disbanded.	Stars in the firmament portray this culture. It's based on individuals whose allegiance to the organisation is overridden by their own individual needs. Barristers' chambers typify this type of culture.

Although elements of all four cultures will be present in every organisation's culture it is likely that one will dominate the others.

HOW TO USE IT

■ Use Handy's questionnaire from the *Gods of Management* (available online) to identify your organisation's culture and any mismatch between it and the type of culture you would like to work in.

■ If you are happy to work in the culture then identify a successful manager within your organisation. Analyse how they behave, and model your behaviours on what they do.

■ In a club culture your authority, power and credibility will depend upon your relationship with the central power source, be that an individual or group. To succeed you have to become a member of the 'in-group' *(see Theory 18)* and do things in a way it approves of.

■ In a role culture the expert who understands the organisation's rules and procedures has tremendous power and influence. Therefore, no matter how boring it is, study the organisation's rules, regulations and procedures and know how to use them to your benefit.

■ Task cultures offer young managers the opportunity to shine. Volunteer to chair any team that reports to the senior management. If you're a senior manager use the establishment of teams as a way of developing and rewarding your own staff *(see Section 4)*.

■ In every organisation there are a few people who believe that the organisation exists for their benefit. Having one or two of these eccentrics around can be useful as they often think outside the box. However, as manager you need to harness their abilities while controlling their excesses.

QUESTIONS TO ASK

■ What is the organisation's dominant culture?

■ What are the implications of the organisation's culture for my management style?

THEORY 41   # DEAL AND KENNEDY'S RISK AND FEEDBACK MODEL

Use to identify the level of risk and feedback that is culturally acceptable in your organisation.

Terrence Deal and Allan Kennedy suggest that the basis of organisational culture is determined by the degrees of risk and speed of feedback which govern how the organisation functions. They identified four distinct types of culture.

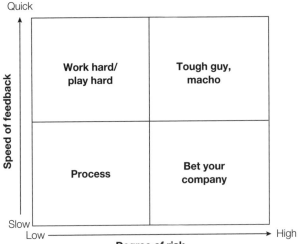

Source: Adapted from Deal, T. E. and Kennedy, A. A., *Corporate Cultures: Rites and Rituals of Corporate Life* (Penguin, 1988) Courtesy of Peters, Fraser & Dunlop.

Work hard/play hard: This is a culture that takes few risks because of issues such as health and safety but needs quick feedback in terms of customer satisfaction.

Tough guy, macho: Includes a world of individualists who regularly take high risks and get quick feedback on whether their actions are right or wrong.

Bet your company: In this culture people take high-risk decisions but they may wait years before they know whether their actions actually paid off.

Process: This can also be described as a bureaucratic culture. It exists where risks are low and feedback is slow.

A well-aligned culture that responds positively to risk and feedback can propel an organisation to success.

HOW TO USE IT

■ List a number of decisions that your organisation has taken in the last 12 to 18 months. Analyse these into low, medium and high risk. Then consider how quickly the organisation expects to receive feedback on the success or failure of each decision. This will give you the organisation's risk feedback profile.

■ Consider what level of risk you are willing to take. This requires more than just a superficial appraisal. Think of any decisions that kept you awake at night. They are a good indicator of the level of risk/ uncertainty you can cope with. Accept these as your benchmark and compare them to the organisation's profile. If you are too cautious or too adventurous for the organisation you should seriously consider packing your bags, unless you can change the organisation's culture *(see Section 5, and Theories 76 and 77)* to match your power to effect change to the risk profile.

■ Provided any gap identified is bridgeable don't mess around. Work out where the differences are between how you act and the behaviour expected by the organisation. Then devise an action plan to close the gaps using the SMART targets *(see Theory 88)*.

■ In your everyday work and dealings with staff model the behaviour expected of managers by the organisation *(see Theory 11)*. If they want a task-focused, hungry young manager who is willing to take risks to get to the top, you have no choice but to give it to them. After all that's what you signed up for.

QUESTIONS TO ASK

■ What types of behaviour gets rewarded in my organisation?

■ Am I comfortable with the level of risk that managers are expected to take? Is it too high or low for me?

THEORY 42 **MORGAN'S ORGANISATIONAL METAPHORS**

Use it to identify how you and your staff feel about the organisation's culture.

Morgan suggests that organisational cultures can be represented as a series of metaphors.

MORGAN'S EIGHT CULTURAL METAPHORS ARE:

Machine: Based upon efficient, standardised and controlled procedures with each unit operating like a cog in a wheel.

Organism: A living system with a life cycle of birth, maturity, death – a matter of survival of the fittest.

Brains: A learning environment involved with information processing with an emphasis on knowledge, intelligence and feedback.

Values: A value-based organisation with an emphasis on tradition, beliefs, history and a shared vision.

Political systems: A culture built on preservation of interests and rights with hidden agendas and alliances.

Psychic prisons: Represents the culture in terms of conscious and unconscious feelings of repression and regression.

Flux and transformation: Sees the culture as a whirlpool of change; sometimes beneficial but sometimes chaotic and paradoxical.

Instruments of domination: Represents a culture that is underpinned by aggression, compliance, exploitation and the imposition of values.

Morgan argues that metaphors create windows into the soul of the organisation and allow us to see, understand and imagine the organisation in different ways.

HOW TO USE IT

- Use Morgan's insights as a starting point for creating your own metaphors. Give staff a sheet of flip-chart paper and ask them to draw a picture of the organisation's culture. Emphasise that you want a picture not an organisation chart.

- In all likelihood you'll get a selection of trees, watering cans, computers, maybe the odd castle under siege. Some of the more interesting ones may include scenes from an inter-galactic war or a teddy bear with fangs and claws (yes, I've had these). Such pictures provide a great insight into how staff perceive the organisation.

- Ask each person what their picture means. Listen to what they say. Identify where the problems lie; for example, the watering can might have a hole in it or maybe a blockage in the spout which prevents the water reaching its intended target. Deal with the issues in the metaphor first and then return to the real world and deal with the real issue. In this case it might mean that important information isn't reaching staff.

- If you're uncomfortable with ambiguity and emotion, metaphors may not be for you. If you are willing to risk it, try it out in a safe environment and see what staff come up with. I bet it will throw up many valuable insights into how they feel about the organisation.

QUESTIONS TO ASK

- Do I believe that everyone in my team shares the same image of the organisation as I do?

- What are the implications of my answer for how I treat staff?

THEORY 43 **GRAVES' CULTURAL LEADERSHIP THEORY**

Use to identify the dominant culture in your organisation.

Desmond Graves argues that organisational culture can be understood by looking at the character of the people who run the organisation. He identifies four possible cultures:

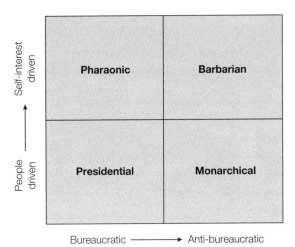

Bureaucratic ⟶ Anti-bureaucratic

Source: Adapted from Graves, D., *Corporate Culture: Diagnosis and Change: Auditing and Changing the Culture of Organizations* (Palgrave Macmillan, 1986).

Pharaonic cultures are dominated by individuals. They are bureaucratic and ego-driven. Cultural leadership is maintained through a passionate respect for status, rituals and order.

Barbarian cultures are dominated by a sense of foreboding. They are ego-driven and anti-bureaucratic. Cultural leadership is maintained through a mixture of uncertainty, terror and charm.

Presidential cultures are bureaucratic and concerned with democracy, status and coordination. Cultural leadership is maintained through consideration of needs and aspirations of the people.

Monarchical cultures are anti-bureaucratic and dominated by a belief in the absolute authority of the leader. Cultural leadership is maintained through the unquestionable loyalty of followers.

In offering these stereotypes, Graves suggests that symbolic leadership is one way of encouraging people that they are working for something worthwhile.

HOW TO USE IT

- As with the discussions on Handy *(see Theory 40)* and Deal and Kennedy *(see Theory 41)* you'll have to identify the culture that is dominant in your organisation and decide if you are happy to remain working there. Use personal reflections to do this.

- Use both personality tests and job interviews to recruit people who can prosper in your organisation's culture.

- If your team or organisation is new, it may have assumed the characteristic of a barbarian culture; one which leans towards a dog-eat-dog approach. This culture is more suited to winning business rather than retaining it. Sooner or later, you will need to modify the culture in order to create stability and structure.

- A Pharaonic culture might favour creativity and imagination but not the emancipation of its workforce. It is one where position and following the correct procedures is likely to be valued. In times of rapid change you will need to adopt a new approach.

- Presidential cultures are less ego-driven than the Barbarian and Pharaonic cultures but status, cooperation and a desire to take into account the needs of the staff can make it slow-moving and cumbersome. In a time of crisis you will have to adopt a more directive approach.

- Monarchical cultures are epitomised by loyalty to the ruler. In many organisations this is the founder. But as the organisation grows it will become impossible for one person to run the show and they will have to share power with others.

QUESTIONS TO ASK

- Does the existing culture serve the needs of the organisation?
- If the culture is inappropriate what changes can I make?

THEORY 44   SCHEIN'S THREE LEVELS OF ORGANISATIONAL CULTURE

Use to understand the role that values and beliefs play in your organisation.

Edgar Schein is generally seen as the foremost thinker on organisational cultures. He claims that the organisational culture is determined by a set of basic beliefs that the organisation has about itself. These beliefs, consciously or subconsciously, define what the organisation is and how it copes with the problems of external competition and internal integration. He argues that the organisation's culture grows out of the legacy of others.

Surface manifestations: These are the artefacts, rituals, myths and legends that send out a message to all concerned about what makes the organisation tick.

Espoused values: These provide a common direction for all employees and a guideline for what is acceptable behaviour.

Basic assumptions: These are the invisible, subconscious and often taken-for-granted understandings held by all employees about the organisation.

Schein's theory suggests that organisations are socially constructed realities that are as much in the minds of staff as they are in the organisation's concrete structures and rules. Therefore to understand the organisation's culture you must understand how the staff see the organisation.

HOW TO USE IT

■ In order to understand your organisation's culture you have to play detective and seek out a range of cultural clues.

■ To identify the surface manifestations ask yourself questions such as: Are workplaces neat and tidy? Do people work in an informal open plan office and wander around talking to each other or do they work in their own offices behind closed doors and communicate through emails? Are meetings lively with animated debates on new ideas or do they follow a strict agenda devised and delivered by those in authority?

■ To identify the organisation's espoused values and basic assumptions, which are buried in people's minds, you will need to talk with them. Workshops are great for this but you need to guarantee confidentiality so that people will feel safe from possible recrimination if they express views that might be unpopular with those in authority. One-to-one interviews may be more suitable provided staff don't feel intimidated by you. You might even think about using a focus group.

■ Once you have collected your data analyse it and use your findings to describe and understand the organisation's culture and identify acceptable and unacceptable behaviours and approaches to management and leadership.

QUESTIONS TO ASK

■ What data do I need to collect to make a judgement about the organisation's culture?

■ What am I going to do with the information produced?

THEORY 45 # JOHNSON AND SCHOLES' CULTURAL WEB

Use this to understand what constitutes appropriate or inappropriate behaviour within your organisation.

Gerry Johnson and Kevan Scholes' cultural web model depicts the culture of an organisation using seven interlinked elements. These elements form a set of behaviours that identify what are considered appropriate or inappropriate behaviour in the organisation.

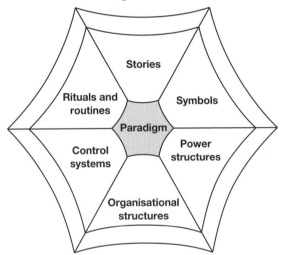

Source: Adapted from Johnson, G., Whittington, R., and Scholes, K., *Exploring Strategy: Text and Cases* (9th edn) (Pearson Education, 2011).

The paradigm is the set of assumptions about the organisation which are taken for granted and shared by everyone.

Rituals and routines describe 'how we do things around here' and how members of the organisation behave towards each other.

Stories are told by members of the organisation to each other, to outsiders, to new recruits etc., and embed the present in the organisation's history.

Symbols are things such as logos, jargon and image that have become a shorthand representation describing the nature of the organisation.

Power structures relates to the real movers and shakers in the organisation. They may be specific individuals, small groups or departments.

Control systems include performance management and reward systems that emphasise what is important in the organisation and focus attention on specific activities.

Structures (Organisational and Power) relate to management hierarchies, reporting systems and decision-making processes.

HOW TO USE IT

■ Use the questions below to review each element of the organisation's cultural web and identify any changes required *(see Section 6)*.

■ What cultural paradigm does the organisation operate in? How much of the organisation's culture is linked to the past? How uniform is it? How long has it been like this? Do I and other managers in the organisation attempt to align the organisation's strategy and culture? Or does the organisational culture 'dictate' strategy rather than management?

■ What rituals do I and others unconsciously follow? What aspects of the way I operate do I take for granted? Do I, or my colleagues, need to change the way we operate?

■ What stories or messages does the organisation tell staff, customers and suppliers? What impression do they create? Ratners, the most successful jeweller in Britain at the time, collapsed overnight when the chairman Gerald Ratner was filmed saying that the reason he could sell a 'gold' necklace for £3.99 was because it was crap. He meant it as a joke but it revealed what the organisation thought of its customers.

■ What messages do the organisation's symbols such as logos, publicity material, website and press releases give out about the organisation?

■ How do the power bases within the organisation impact on my capacity to function effectively? *(See Theories 55 and 77.)*

■ Use the above information when dealing with staff, colleagues and senior management to answer their questions in culturally acceptable terms. You will also know when, where and how to lob a cultural hand grenade into the mix when it's required and is to your benefit.

QUESTIONS TO ASK

■ What are the great unwritten rules of my organisation?

■ In whose interest is it to maintain the current organisational culture?

THEORY 46 # HOFSTEDE'S SIX CROSS-ORGANISATIONAL DIMENSIONS

Use as a checklist when you are engaged in changing organisational culture.

Geert Hofstede suggests that there are six dimensions which can be used to describe the organisation's culture. He poses these as a series of opposites and asks the user to plot where their organisation is on each of the six continuums.

HOFSTEDE'S SIX DIMENSIONS ARE:

Process vs result: Process-oriented cultures are low risk and low effort. Results-oriented cultures welcome change and challenge and are high effort.

Person vs job: A person-driven culture places employee welfare at the heart of the organisation. A job-driven culture emphasises completion of tasks over regard for the staff.

Parochial vs professional: Staff working in a parochial culture display the same characteristics at work as they do at home. Those in a professional culture differentiate how they act at home and work.

Open systems vs closed systems: Open cultures welcome newcomers and outsiders. New people joining closed cultures struggle to gain acceptance.

Loose vs tight control: In a loose control culture, working practices are flexible and things such as dress codes and timekeeping are relaxed. Tight control cultures allow very little leeway on issues such as working place practices and behaviour.

Normative vs pragmatic: In a normative culture there is strict adherence to rules, regulations and procedures. A pragmatic culture allows flexibility in following procedures if it means customer needs can be met.

HOW TO USE IT

■ If you decide to move from a process-driven to a results-driven culture, don't overwhelm people with too many challenges. If your change is in the opposite direction ensure that high performers don't get bored by a lack of challenge.

■ Sensitivity may be required if employees, who have been used to an employee-oriented culture, are asked to be more job-focused. But don't molly-coddle those moving in the opposite direction as they may find such treatment uncomfortable.

■ Some people with well-organised home lives may bring those disciplines to work. Their parochial way of doing things might be better than what you've got and forcing a professional approach on them may be counter-productive.

■ Look out for the people used to working in a closed system culture. In extreme circumstances, they may think that they are the 'chosen ones'. They will be suspicious of people moving into their domain and if they are moving into an open culture they may be overwhelmed and a bit suspicious of the welcoming nature of their new colleagues.

■ People used to informality in dress code and general behaviour may find it difficult to accept a more formal environment. The same is true of those moving in the opposite direction. Give both groups time to adjust.

■ People moving from a pragmatic to a normative culture and vice versa will need to come to terms with the differences in expectations regarding following rules and procedures. Make it absolutely clear what these are and what's expected of staff.

QUESTIONS TO ASK

■ Why do I want to change the organisation's culture?
■ What are the benefits of changing the culture?

THEORY 47 # HARGREAVES AND BALKANISED CULTURES

Use to strengthen team spirit in your organisation.

Hargreaves, writing in the context of education, noticed that while a school or college would have a single over-riding culture many individual departments had very distinct cultures. For example, the culture in Arts and Humanities was very different to that which existed in Science or Engineering faculties. He likened this to the Balkans where, to an outsider, there can appear to be a fairly uniform culture shared by numerous states but when examined closely each state has a very distinct culture.

THE FIVE KEY FEATURES OF BALKANISED CULTURES ARE:

Each division, department or team (sub-group) sees itself as a separate entity from the rest of the organisation.

Over time each sub-group develops its own unique culture.

There is 'low permeability' between the cultures of different groups. With each group erecting walls to keep out the influences of others.

Once these barriers have been erected it's difficult to breach or remove them.

Over time people become attached to the identity of their sub-group and develop a set of self-interests that they actively promote even when they conflict with the good of the whole organisation.

Although focused on education, the model is clearly applicable to any large-scale organisation. For instance, just look at the very different cultures that exist within the accounts and sales departments of any organisation.

HOW TO USE IT

■ Use this as a theory to strengthen the team spirit within your group. Start by talking up the differences between you and other sub-groups in the organisation. Differentiate your team from the rest of the herd and encourage the development of traditions and practices that are unique to your team.

■ Encourage your team to think of themselves as different, even special. Make your people feel proud to belong to the best team in the organisation and promote the idea that only the best get into your gang.

■ Remember, everyone likes a bit of competition. Establish a friendly rivalry with other groups in the organisation and celebrate when you 'beat' them – even if the other group didn't know they were in a contest.

■ While you want your team to think of themselves as special, they must understand that it's no good if they win but the organisation loses. Their ultimate loyalty has to be to the organisation. Don't fall into the trap of sub-optimisation.

■ Think about Balkanised cultures whenever you move jobs within your organisation. Take time to discover your new team's culture. Only when you understand it and have evaluated its strengths and weaknesses should you consider changing or destroying it.

QUESTIONS TO ASK

■ What Balkanised cultures exist within the organisation?

■ How can I use the idea of Balkanised cultures to improve my team's results?

A FINAL WORD ON ORGANISATIONAL CULTURE THEORIES

WHY HANDY WAS CROWNED AS KING

I chose Handy because thanks to the questionnaire that accompanies it you can obtain a quick overview of the organisational culture that you operate in and some measure of how well that culture suits you. No other theory gives you that much information for so little effort. The better you know yourself and your organisation the more accurate the results will be. Even if you have only been working in the organisation for a short period of time you can still get some useful information from the questionnaire.

To unlock the mystery of your organisation's culture you need to read the cultural clues. So watch, listen and only then ask questions or enter into a debate. Because organisational culture is multi-faceted you need to collect data from people throughout the organisation as well as customers and suppliers. Use as many different ways to collect data as possible. If you limit the amount of information you use you run the risk of basing your findings on biased, incomplete and selective data. So, get out of your office and try a bit of Management by Walking About *(see Theory 10)*.

One way to access other people's view of the organisation's culture is to get them to draw a picture. Their picture will reveal far more than any questionnaire or essay that they might write on the subject and they'll find it fun – even if they think you're some kind of weirdo to ask them do it. But hey, staff like eccentric managers. The results will surprise you. I guarantee that in a group of ten people at least one will come up with something totally unexpected. That's inevitable because 'There's now't so queer as folk' and it's folk that create organisational culture, not just managers.

Before you try to change your organisation's culture ask for whose benefit you are doing it. Just because you don't like something doesn't mean it needs changing. Changing any organisation's culture is always a risk and not something to undertake on a whim. It's entirely possible that the organisation's culture does not need to be changed. Remember the story of the proud mum at her son's army passing-out parade exclaiming that everyone was out of step except her Jimmy. Well, maybe they were – maybe it is the others that need to change to match your preferred culture, but can you afford to be wrong? The old adage 'If it ain't broke don't fix it' may be relevant here.

If you want your organisation to progress you need to identify the organisation's existing culture, what culture is required for the organisation to flourish in the future, and, if a change is required, how you are going to bring about the required change. Don't start tinkering until you have answers for all three questions.

Finally, remember that any medium-sized or larger organisation is likely to consist of several sub-cultures. Such a set-up can help build team spirit, but all sub-cultures must contribute to the welfare of the organisation not weaken it. Remember that to change the organisation's culture all you may need to do is change just one powerful sub-culture.

SECTION 6

HOW TO
MANAGE
CHANGE

INTRODUCTION

The question 'How do you eat an elephant?' is usually answered by the response 'One bite at a time'. (Don't write in complaining; I love elephants just as much as you.) This was never truer than in the approach you need to take to deliver a successful change. Change is a long-drawn-out process that can't be forced on people. Rush it and you'll pay a hefty price.

All change evokes the emotions of fear and panic as well as of excitement and anticipation. Each person perceives change differently. What is fresh and stimulating to one person is terrifying to the next. People also differ in their ability to face the unknown and deal with the uncertainty that change brings. I don't think for one minute that this section will deal with all of the issues you'll face as someone managing a change process. What it will do is give you a greater understanding of the problems that people have at different stages in the process and some useful ideas to help you manage people under stress.

The one message that seems to override all others is the need for good communication during periods of change. Good communication requires managers to spend more time listening to staff than talking at them. Like the Englishman abroad, too many managers think that if they speak S-L-O-W-L-Y and L-O-U-D-L-Y enough they will be understood.

As an example of what happens if you misread external trends consider the following. Developments in information technology have created a world where people can now communicate on a level they couldn't have dreamed possible less than a decade ago and fortunes have been made and lost in IT over the last 40 years. A shame then for the young computer studies graduate of the 1970s who spurned a career in IT claiming that computers were 'just a flash in the pan' and there was no career to be had in IT. Well, I was only 21 at the time.

Change is about what's happening all around you and you need to be constantly reviewing both your internal and external environment for trends that can impact on you and your organisation.

Always carry out a post-evaluation of any change and do this regardless of the outcome. Knowing why something worked well is just as valuable as knowing why something failed. You can then use the information gathered to inform your next change project.

THEORY 48 KÜBLER-ROSS'S CHANGE CYCLE

Use to track people's journey through any significant change and remember that until everyone has reached acceptance your job isn't done.

Elisabeth Kübler-Ross's five-stage change cycle was intended to help people deal with bereavement but has since been adapted to reflect the stages of any major change event including changes at work.

Denial: This is the initial stage of numbness and shock provoking a sense of disbelief. It can produce either a conscious or unconscious refusal to accept what is happening.

Anger: When acceptance of the reality of the situation takes place, denial turns to anger, either through self-recrimination or anger with others.

Bargaining: This is intended to either resolve the problem faced by the person or put off the inevitable.

Depression: This stage reached if bargaining has failed and it is at this point that the reality of the situation sets in and emotions such as sadness, regret and loss are felt.

Acceptance: Dealing with sadness and regret is a necessary pre-requisite for acceptance. Acceptance is reached once the individual realises that the change is permanent.

Kübler-Ross warns that people don't move through the stages in a well-ordered sequential manner. They may stall at a particular stage or even regress to a previous stage. Such regression may be an essential part of the process before the ultimate state of acceptance is reached.

HOW TO USE IT

■ Discuss the proposed change with staff as early as possible. This will give them a sense of ownership and control over events and build trust between you and them.

■ Remember change may be exciting for you but for many it's terrifying. People fear the unknown and worry that they will lose status and won't be able to cope in the new world *(see Theory 23)*. To help staff overcome their fears provide support at every stage of the process by providing opportunities for staff to discuss their fears, options and opportunities with you or another supervisor.

■ Remember, people move through the change cycle at different speeds. They may even get stuck at a particular stage or be thrown back to an earlier stage by events. Be on the lookout for such people and offer support and assistance.

■ Communicate with staff every which way you can. Don't restrict communications to formal meetings. Use MBWA *(see Theory 10)* to find out what staff feel and think. Answer questions fully. If you don't know the answer say 'I'll get back to you within 24 hours'. Always deliver on your promises and don't try and bluff your way out of a problem. Staff don't trust managers that spread organic fertiliser for a living.

■ Appoint change champions *(see Theory 53)* from frontline staff. They can respond to queries instantaneously, stop rumours and misinformation from spreading and act as a link between you and the front line.

■ Allow staff opportunities to discuss their fears and concerns openly and provide all staff with training as early as possible. This will reduce the fear of the unknown and build confidence.

QUESTIONS TO ASK

■ Who can I rely on for help and support?

■ Who is likely to oppose me?

THEORY 49 # SHEWHART'S PLAN–DO–CHECK–ACT (PDCA) MODEL

Use this model as the basis for any change event.

Walter Shewhart developed his model in the 1930s and it was widely used by Deming *(see Theory 68)* and many others to implement quality improvement programmes. However, it can apply to numerous business situations. The cycle is a systematic approach which emphasises that any change to a system or process, no matter how large or small, must pass through four stages.

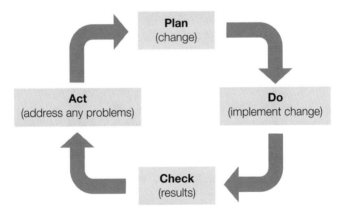

Shewhart's cycle allows managers to anticipate and tackle problems in a structured, disciplined, logical and sequential manner.

HOW TO USE IT

■ Use evaluative tools, such as Ishikawa's fishbone or Pareto analysis *(see Theories 72 and 81)*, to find out what needs to be improved and identify possible solutions. Involve others in the planning process and don't be afraid if some blue sky thinking occurs. After all, who would have thought that putting bits of coloured glass in the middle of roads would save countless thousands of lives? But don't fall into the trap of paralysis by analysis.

■ Once you have some idea of what you want to do, undertake a few small-scale experiments to test out whether the changes will work or not. Do your experiments with small groups so as to minimise disruption and communicate with staff before, during and after the experiment.

■ Check if the small-scale changes achieved the desired results? If they did then progress to the Do stage and implement your change. If not, don't be afraid to admit failure, learn from what has happened and go back to the Plan stage and start thinking about alternative solutions.

■ Check/evaluate the impact of the change you have made. Use your findings to identify any problems/weaknesses in what you have done and act to rectify them.

■ Remember, change involves risk. Have the guts to do what you think needs doing. There is nothing more destructive to staff morale than to see time and effort wasted by managers too scared to run with a great idea.

QUESTIONS TO ASK

■ How detailed/realistic is my change plan?

■ Is the plan achievable with the skills and resources available to me?

THEORY 50   # LEWIN'S UNFREEZE–CHANGE–REFREEZE MODEL

Use to remind you of the need to reduce people's resistance to change by challenging (unfreezing) their current locked-in views before embarking on implementing the change.

Kurt Lewin produced one of the cornerstone models for managing change. He uses the analogy of changing the shape of a block of ice from a cube to a cone to describe the model. To do this, you must firstly melt the ice cube (unfreeze), then mould the new shape (change) before finally solidifying the cone (refreeze).

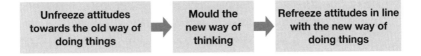

| Unfreeze attitudes towards the old way of doing things | ➡ | Mould the new way of thinking | ➡ | Refreeze attitudes in line with the new way of doing things |

Lewin argues that by following the three-step process you motivate people to want change, empower them to contribute to the change process and finally re-establish a sense of stability within the organisation.

HOW TO USE IT

■ Both before and during any change process be prepared to challenge the beliefs, values and behaviours that may inhibit change.

■ Before you start the unfreezing process identify what changes you want to make and why they are necessary *(see Section 7)*.

■ Win the support of key people from all levels within the organisation by creating a compelling argument in favour of change *(see Theory 55)*. You may have to vary the argument depending on who you talk to. Those in charge of the money will want to see financial gains, whilst human resources will want to see a positive impact on personnel. Improved working conditions will be music to the ears of the staff and unions.

■ Keep staff informed of progress every step of the way. This will motivate the eager and help you deal with the rational and irrational fears of the worried *(see Theories 10 and 48)*.

■ Understanding what benefits the change will bring is a critical factor in moving the change process along. Support people as they embed the changes into their everyday working practices. Only when the changes are in place, and you feel confident that they will bring long-term benefits to the organisation, should you begin the process of refreezing.

QUESTIONS TO ASK

■ To create a positive buzz about the project what early success can I promote as good news stories for both the staff and organisation?

■ What answers will I use to combat negative arguments against the change from stakeholders, staff, colleagues and senior management?

THEORY 51   LEWIN'S FORCE FIELD ANALYSIS

Use prior knowledge of the issue to identify the forces in play that support or resist change and to develop a strategy for driving change forward.

Like other aspects of Kurt Lewin's work *(see Theory 50)* the basic idea behind force field analysis is simple; it's only in its application that you can truly appreciate how profound his idea is. His analysis involves identifying two sets of factors, those which support change (drivers) and those that oppose it (resistors). By determining the strength of each factor it is possible to 'calculate' whether a change is likely to be successful or not.

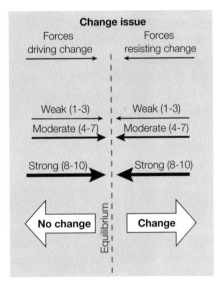

Representing the strength by the thickness of the arrows or allocating a score to each will help with the analysis.

HOW TO USE IT

■ Assemble a team of around four or five people to help you identify the drivers for change and the resistors to change *(see Section 4)*.

■ Don't be fazed if the same issue is considered by some as a driver and by others a resistor. This will be down to individual perspective.

■ Take an A3 sheet of paper. Describe the change proposed and record this in a box – top centre of the sheet. From the bottom of the box draw a line down the middle of the page.

■ List the drivers for change in the left-hand column and the resistors to change in the right-hand column. You might use a SWOT and/or PEST analysis for this *(see Theories 65 and 66)*.

■ Score each force. For example, assign a score of 1 (weak) to 10 (strong) to each force/resistor. For added visual effect draw horizontal arrows for each force/resistor towards the centre line (the bolder the arrow the greater the force).

■ Clearly, the score allocated to each factor is subjective. That's why you should involve others. Debate the strength of each force/resistor and either agree a single score or take an average of the scores given by the team.

■ Add up the scores on each side of the line. A quick glance should tell you whether change is a done deal (drivers far outweigh resistors), a dead duck (resistors far outweighing drivers) or a difficult decision (little to choose between the two).

■ If it's a close call and you still want to go ahead with the change then develop a strategy that will enable you to strengthen the forces, weaken the resistors or both.

QUESTIONS TO ASK

■ Who can help me identify the driving and resisting forces?

■ Have I selected both advocates and opponents of the change in the team?

THEORY 52 **KOTTER'S EIGHT-STEP APPROACH TO CHANGE**

Use this to appreciate that building the proper foundations for change is essential. Don't go off half-cocked.

John Kotter argued that 70% of all major change programmes failed due to a lack of careful planning. He devised an eight-step process for dealing with this.

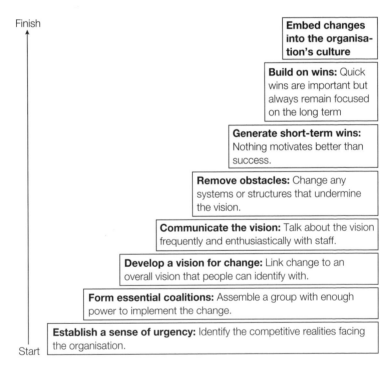

Finish

Start

Embed changes into the organisation's culture

Build on wins: Quick wins are important but always remain focused on the long term

Generate short-term wins: Nothing motivates better than success.

Remove obstacles: Change any systems or structures that undermine the vision.

Communicate the vision: Talk about the vision frequently and enthusiastically with staff.

Develop a vision for change: Link change to an overall vision that people can identify with.

Form essential coalitions: Assemble a group with enough power to implement the change.

Establish a sense of urgency: Identify the competitive realities facing the organisation.

Kotter stresses that hard work, careful planning and building the proper foundations for change are essential to improve the chances of an effective change management programme.

HOW TO USE IT

- Talk to everyone affected by the change about the implications of failing to take advantage of opportunities or deal with threats faced by the organisation *(see Theories 65 and 66).*

- The support of senior management is essential to any change *(see Theory 55).* Identify who they are and get them onside.

- You will have to articulate your vision *(see Theories 20–22)* to a lot of people at different levels in the organisation. You must be able to express it in a single sentence. Remember, it's the vision not the detail you are selling.

- Don't be fazed if not everyone thinks the vision is for them. Address people's concerns and anxieties through good communication and training. Try everything you can to get them on board but if all of your efforts fail then you may have to exclude them from the process.

- Look for a few inexpensive, sure-fire quick wins. Reward people who help you get these wins but be careful of claiming successful change too early. To misquote Churchill, quick wins are not the beginning of the end but merely the end of the beginning.

- When you do succeed, celebrate the achievement and make sure that everyone's contribution is suitably recognised.

QUESTIONS TO ASK

- Does my plan for change take into account all eight stages?
- How am I going to publicise quick wins?

THEORY 53 **MOSS KANTER AND CHANGE MASTERS (CROWN AS QUEEN)**

Use this to identify the abilities you need when managing change.

Rosabeth Moss Kanter is rightly regarded as one of the great innovators in change theory. She uses the term Change Masters to describe managers who are at the forefront of change within their organisations and suggests that they all share the same seven abilities.

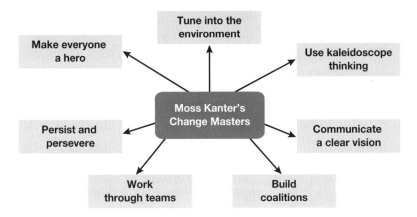

Change masters:

- **tune into the environment** and identify new opportunities, threats and ideas before others;

- **use kaleidoscope thinking** and encourage staff to indulge in blue sky thinking;

- **communicate a clear vision** and inspire others to become excited by their vision;

- **build coalitions** and enlist the support of others;

- **work through teams** and get the commitment of everyone whose efforts are required to make the vision a reality;

- **persist and persevere** and are not discouraged by obstacles and problems;

- **make everyone a hero** by celebrating achievements and acknowledge all contributions that helped make the change work.

Moss Kanter argues that effective change masters should, firstly, focus on tasks where the emphasis is on results not procedures; secondly, organise people into teams with complete responsibility for their part of the end product; and, finally, create an atmosphere which emphasises the value of the people involved.

HOW TO USE IT

- Work with a small group of people to examine what new ideas, opportunities and threats face the organisation *(see Theories 65 and 66)*. Encourage the team to indulge in blue sky thinking and challenge assumptions that hinder progress. Canvass other staff for their ideas about what needs to change. Make sure that all ideas are acknowledged.

- Identify what changes need to be made and put together your change plan *(see Section 7)*.

- Communicate a clear vision for change and use it to inspire others while building coalitions and enlisting the support of others *(see Theory 55)*.

- In a large project organise people into sub-teams and give them complete responsibility for their part of the job.

- If you have just one team, ensure that members own the project and don't expect you to be responsible for everything. They must take responsibility for their part of the project *(see Section 4)*.

- At first, focus on tasks which produce concrete results not procedures. This will give the team something tangible to celebrate and undermine the doubters.

- Don't be discouraged by obstacles and problems. Managing the difficult middle section of any project is hard. The change is underway, when suddenly resources dry up, obstacles arise and critics crawl out of the woodwork. Morale sags and momentum slows down. That's the time to follow Churchill's advice and 'Keep Buggering On'.

- On completion, celebrate everyone's achievements and acknowledge all contributions that helped make the change work.

QUESTIONS TO ASK

- How am I going to create an atmosphere in which team members feel valued?

- Which of the seven activities listed by Moss Kanter am I going to find most difficult? What am I going to do to deal with this?

THEORY 54 | # BURKE–LITWIN'S DRIVERS FOR CHANGE

Use this theory as a starting point to identify and understand the different dimensions that you have to take into account if you are to plan for and implement a successful change.

Warner Burke and George Litwin's change model looks at 12 organisational dimensions that are key to change. The dimensions are organised into four levels and each dimension is explored using a series of questions. Failure to deal with the content of each dimension will impede or stop change.

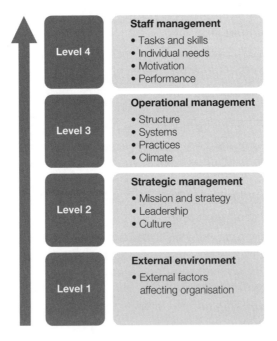

Level 4

Staff management
- Tasks and skills
- Individual needs
- Motivation
- Performance

Level 3

Operational management
- Structure
- Systems
- Practices
- Climate

Level 2

Strategic management
- Mission and strategy
- Leadership
- Culture

Level 1

External environment
- External factors affecting organisation

HOW TO USE IT

This theory requires you to ask a series of questions at each level. Based on the answers received you must decide what change is required and develop a suitable implementation strategy. The following questions are prompts only and you need to develop questions specific to your organisation under each heading.

- **Level 1 The environment:** What are the political, economic, social and technological developments prompting change *(see Theory 66)*?

- **Level 2 Strategic management:** How does the change fit into the organisation's vision and mission *(see Section 7)*? Who is driving the change? Do the organisation's beliefs, values and assumptions embrace or reject change *(see Section 5)*?

- **Level 3 Operational management:** Do the various power bases in the organisation support change *(see Theory 55 and Section 9)*? Do the organisation's policies and procedures support change? Do current working practices support change? Are the staff receptive to change?

- **Level 4 Staff management:** Does the staff have the skills to support change? Will the change address both organisational and individual needs? Are staff motivated enough to make the change work and perform well after it *(see Section 3)*?

Once you have answers to the above you can start to plan your change.

QUESTIONS TO ASK

- What specific questions, relevant to my organisation, do I need to ask under each heading?
- Who can help me to identify and answer the questions?

THEORY 55 EGAN'S SHADOW-SIDE THEORY

Use this to develop strategies for dealing with the different stakeholders who may support or hinder your change plans.

Gerard Egan argues that different approaches need to be taken to manage different stakeholders within an organisation. He categorises the stakeholders as follows:

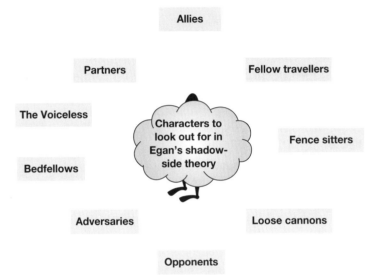

Allies: Those who, if encouraged sufficiently, will support you.

Fellow travellers: Those who support the agenda for change but not necessarily you.

Fence sitters: Those whose allegiances are unclear, even to themselves.

Loose cannons: Those who you have no idea of which way they'll jump.

Opponents: Those who oppose the agenda for change but have nothing against you personally.

Adversaries: Those who oppose you and the agenda for change.

Bedfellows: Those who support the agenda but may not trust you.

The voiceless: Those who have little or no power to support or oppose the agenda for change.

Partners: Those who support the agenda for change.

Egan describes working on the 'shadow-side' as a way of dealing with stakeholders who can't be dealt with using the organisation's usual practices. Partners and Allies need to be kept onside, whereas Opponents and Adversaries may have to be discredited or marginalised. Fence sitters and the Voiceless should be seduced to ensure they don't go over to the other side.

HOW TO USE IT

- Recognise the role that the organisation's stakeholders play in the success of major change events.

- Recognise that this theory is concerned with organisational politics (see Section 9) and that without some political savvy you'll 'get done' by those who play the game better.

- Identify and get to know the key stakeholders in your organisation. Do this even if you don't envisage making a change in the near future. Work out what power, influence and interests each stakeholder has.

- Identify those stakeholders that might have an impact on your project. Rank them in terms of possible impact. The stakeholder with low power and low interest needn't take up too much of your time. It's those with high power and high interest that you have to engage with and develop as allies (see Theory 62).

- Continue to keep a watchful eye on the others and brief them regularly, but remember where your priorities lie.

- Get to know how each stakeholder feels about your change agenda and you personally. This will help you deal with them. Socialising with people you don't particularly like may be a chore but the odd drink outside of work may save hours of work in the office and at formal meetings.

- Remember, as the agenda for change rolls out it will affect more people. In focusing on the Opponents and Adversaries don't lose sight of the importance of consolidating your Partners and Allies.

- As the change progresses, monitor what the Fence sitters, Loose cannons and the Voiceless are doing. If they suddenly side with the opposition it could prove disastrous for you.

QUESTIONS TO ASK

- Have I identified all the stakeholders connected to the change?
- Do I know which stakeholders I need to concentrate my efforts on?

A FINAL WORD ON CHANGE MANAGEMENT THEORIES

WHY ROSABETH MOSS KANTER WAS CROWNED AS QUEEN

I love Egan's shadow-side theory. It plays into my James Bond fantasies and addresses a complex area in a clear and coherent way but Rosabeth Moss Kanter just beat him to the crown.

Moss Kanter's theory is actually two theories for the price of one. Read the list of abilities that a change agent requires and you can quickly identify areas where you need to improve your own skills. But add to that her advice on what a manager needs to prioritise when leading change and she jumps clear of the competition. If you only ever read one book on change read her *The Change Masters* (1989).

It's worth remembering that after death, divorce and moving house, changing jobs is about as stressful as it gets. A major change in your current job isn't far behind that. Keep this in mind when dealing with staff. Adults learn from their experiences. If a member of your staff had a bad experience of change they are likely to fear any change you propose. If their experience of change was exciting and successful they will probably think that you are moving too slowly and you'll have to rein them in. The only way you will know how they feel is if you keep your mouth shut and your ears open. Talk to your staff, don't just talk at them, and listen to what they have to say.

While it might be tempting to rush into change and complete it as quickly as possible, remember that you can only move at the speed of the slowest member of staff. The *Titanic* went too fast and hit an iceberg. If you rush change it's almost guaranteed that you'll hit your very own iceberg, which may have disastrous consequences for your career.

While there is a certain truth in the claim that if you can dream it then it can be built, it's difficult to build anything substantial without the help of others. Therefore, when making your case for change ensure that you can summarise your vision for change in a sentence. It's that single sentence your listeners will remember and hopefully get behind the idea.

You can never control change entirely. But if you wait for change to be forced upon you by events you will have no control over it. Therefore, anticipate what changes are required and deal with them at a time you choose and on your terms, rather than be buffeted by events.

If you know that change is inevitable, then part of your strategy for dealing with it should involve getting to know, understand and influence the stakeholders in your organisation *(see Theories 55 and 62)*. It is they who have the power to help or block any changes you may wish to make. It's easier to develop these relationships when you want nothing from the stakeholders rather than when you are in the middle of a change and desperate for their support. So start building those relationships at the beginning of the change process.

Finally always remember you can learn just as much from your failures as your successes.

SECTION 7

STRATEGIC MANAGEMENT

INTRODUCTION

In any competitive environment the difference between winning and losing is often the quality of planning. The GB Cycling Team is renowned for the meticulous planning of its director David Brailsford. The team has been so successful since he took over that there have been dark mutterings by other counties about the use of drugs and even tiny motors in the hubs of wheels. The French in particular couldn't believe that Britain's improvement was down to exceptional preparation and planning, and at a meeting with David one of the French team pressed him hard to reveal the secret of Britain's success. Fed up with the incessant questioning David looked over his shoulder, leaned forward and whispered, 'The truth is we use really round wheels'. It seemed to satisfy the Frenchman.

People find it hard to believe that good planning can significantly improve performance. Yet the same people are happy to subscribe to the belief that 'poor planning produces p*** poor performance'. There is clearly an inconsistency in people's logic.

Don't get me wrong, strategic planning won't solve all your problems. Planning can never be entirely accurate because it involves prediction and no one can tell you what's going to happen tomorrow let alone next year. However, the act of planning requires you to think about the future and consider what might happen and how you will deal with different eventualities should they arise. That in itself is valuable. Planning also provides you with a road map of where you want to go. Yes, events may require you to make a detour and road closures and traffic jams may disrupt your journey. But if you know your final destination you can constantly update your route even if that means you have to go via Cardiff to get to London from Birmingham (if the M6 road works don't end soon this may be the quickest route).

There are two types of plan that you will almost certainly be involved in, namely business and strategic. A business plan usually covers a period of one year whereas a rolling strategic plan may cover three to five years. Personally I think any plan over three years contains more conjecture and wishful thinking than useful information. If you don't think that you are involved in strategic or business planning then I bet you either control or work to a budget. Well, a budget is a business plan with a price ticket on it. And if it isn't then it's not a very good budget. Too often, the budget drives the business plan when what you really require is a realistic business plan which, when costed, becomes the budget.

The theories discussed in this part will help you understand and contribute to either the business or strategic planning cycle in your organisation. Depending on your level in the organisation some will be more useful to you than others. However, all of them will provide you with different ways of looking at your organisation. The knowledge and understanding gained from this will make you a better manager and prepare you for further promotion.

If it's not already obvious from the above, having an effective operational strategy will ensure that the day-to-day decisions you make regarding your customers, competitors, people and products/services are in the best long-term interests of your organisation. This knowledge will help you to make strategic decisions that are both defensible and economically attractive for your organisation.

Finally, to be effective a good strategy should encourage everyone in the organisation to work together to achieve a common aim. Therefore it should not be imposed on staff. Rather, staff at all levels should be able to contribute to it and in doing so own it.

THEORY 56

JOHNSON AND SCHOLES' SEVEN STAGES OF STRATEGIC PLANNING

Use as a summary of the major stages in any planning process.

Gerry Johnson and Kevan Scholes suggest that there are seven stages in any planning process. These are:

Finish

Reward: On successful implementation of the plan, recognise the efforts of all involved.

Control: Set up a system to compare actual with planned performance. Take action to correct under-performance. But be prepared to alter the plan in light of changing conditions.

Actions and tasks: Identify the steps that individuals and teams must take to complete and execute the strategy.

Strategies: Identify the actions that must be taken to achieve objectives.

Objectives: Break down the goals into specific and measurable objectives that can be monitored.

Goals: Identify what goals must be achieved for the organisation to realise its vision.

Start

Mission: Identify the organisation's vision. What does it want to achieve?

HOW TO USE IT

- Use the seven-stage approach as a valuable overview of the stages that you need to go through if you are to produce a comprehensive and well-thought-out plan.

- Different writers define the terms' aims, goals and objectives differently and others use the terms interchangeably. Always make certain that in any conversation or meeting you have that everyone shares a common set of definitions.

- Identify which planning approach your organisation favours – top down or bottom up. Based on this identify the role management expects you to play *(see Theories 57–59).*

- Top-down approaches involve senior managers and a few 'planning experts' locking themselves away for a week and developing a plan with little reference to anyone else. In this case the role of middle manager is to accept what has been produced and implement it without question. If this is your organisation's approach your job is to sell the plan to staff, even if you don't personally support the plan.

- Bottom-up approaches involve collecting data from staff at every level and senior managers and planners using this to draw up the strategic plan. The role of the middle manager is to collect, analyse and summarise the most useful data before reporting it to the planning team. There will be more work for you in terms of feeding into the plan but implementation will be easier as staff will feel that their views were listened to.

- Whatever your role, use one or two trusted staff to help you provide information/implement the plan.

QUESTIONS TO ASK

- Do I prefer top-down or bottom-up approaches to planning?
- Are there any differences between the organisation's preferred approach and mine? If so, how am I going to resolve them?

THEORY 57   ANSOFF'S MODERNIST
             APPROACH TO STRATEGIC
             MANAGEMENT

Use if you find yourself in an organisation that believes in top-down planning.

It is important to realise that Igor Ansoff's approach to strategic management was developed in the 1960s after nearly two decades of growth and stability in the USA. It was based upon the belief that by scientific analysis of available information, it was possible to identify the future strategic direction of the company and plan for it accordingly.

THE MODERNIST APPROACH TO STRATEGIC MANAGEMENT SUGGESTS THAT:

Senior management, supported by specialist planners, are responsible for the analysis of the current and future prospects of the organisation and the development of a strategic plan.

The results of the planning process can be accurate over a three- to ten-year cycle but that accuracy declines as the planning horizon is extended further.

When unexpected events occur, management must react quickly and update the strategic plan as required. It is to guard against the danger of the unknown that Ansoff argues that all organisations should have as an aim the ability to remain flexible.

Staff will accept and implement the plan that is passed down to them and that implementation will be achieved without difficulty.

HOW TO USE IT

■ Identify which planning paradigm your organisation favours *(see Theories 58 and 59)*.

■ If you work in a modernist paradigm consider how you can ensure that information you and your staff hold is passed on to the planners and not ignored by those who 'think they know best'. This will improve the quality of information available to the planners and protect your team against bad decisions made because of poor information.

■ Knowing that senior management think that the implementation of the finalised plan is non-problematic, devise an implementation strategy that will motivate and support your staff during the plan's roll-out *(see Section 3)*.

■ Devise an early warning system that will alert you to the need to change the plan because of changes in the internal or external environment *(see Theories 65–67)*.

■ Have in place a reporting system that will allow you to report your concerns to those responsible for amending the plan. Be prepared to argue your case. Planners are often loath to admit that they got it wrong.

QUESTIONS TO ASK

■ Am I part of the 'planning elite'? If so, how am I going to gain staff commitment to the plan?

■ If I'm not a part of the 'planning elite' how can I influence their decisions?

PETERS AND WATERMAN'S POST-MODERNIST APPROACH TO STRATEGIC MANAGEMENT

THEORY 58

Use if your organisation believes that it is impossible to plan for the future and that the manager's job is to prepare staff to react quickly to constant change.

Unlike Ansoff, Tom Peters and Robert Waterman were writing in the 1980s. The 1970s' economic upheaval caused by two oil crises, a changing political landscape and the arrival of new technologies ushered in an era of constant change.

THE POST-MODERNIST APPROACH TO STRATEGIC MANAGEMENT SUGGESTS THAT:

It's impossible to predict the future. No longer can change be extrapolated from past events. According to them, change has become discontinuous and unpredictable and planning has to reflect this new reality.

Planning now involves the identification of new ideas and trends as they occur and quickly mobilising the resources required to capitalise upon such opportunities.

The role of senior managers is to support, develop and run with the ideas of middle managers and frontline staff because only they are in a position to know what the customer wants and predict the latest market trends.

As unexpected chance events are now the norm, organisations have to be willing to turn on a dime to deal with the ever-changing demands of customers. To achieve this, staff need to exhibit flexibility, spontaneity and creativity when reacting to customers' demands and changing market circumstances.

HOW TO USE IT

■ Identify which planning paradigm your organisation favours *(see Theories 57 and 59)*.

■ If your organisation believes in the discontinuous nature of change and that traditional planning is useless then create some certainty for yourself and your team by planning for possible changes in advance *(see Theories 65–67)*.

■ Talk to frontline staff, customers, suppliers and competitors to stay abreast of what's 'bubbling under' in the marketplace *(see Theory 8)*.

■ Use scenario planning *(see Theory 67)* to briefly outline what you will do when an issue 'boils over'.

■ To deal with truly unpredictable events train and develop your staff to show flexibility, spontaneity and creativity when reacting to changing circumstances.

■ Record the actions and strategies you use to reduce the effect of uncertainty on your staff. Report these to the senior management as a way of disseminating good practice in the organisation *(see Section 6)*.

QUESTIONS TO ASK

■ Are the changes I face now really greater than those faced by managers between 1914 and 1945?

■ What training do I need to provide to staff? Will traditional management training work or do I need to think about creativity training and the use of role play and simulation?

THEORY 59 QUINN, HAMEL AND PRAHALAD: THE NEW MODERNIST APPROACH

Use if your organisation adopts a middle-of-the-road approach to strategic planning.

The apparent chaos that post-modernist planning implied was challenged by a number of writers in the 1990s. Quinn, Hamel and Prahalad suggested that what was required was an amalgam of the modernist and post-modernist approaches.

THE NEW MODERNIST APPROACH TO STRATEGIC MANAGEMENT SUGGESTS THAT:

Senior management is responsible for intellectual leadership. They collect ideas from staff and combine them with foresight, small-scale experiments and customer feedback to identify the best way forward. They recognise that all plans are based upon inadequate information and therefore they will have to be updated to reflect changing realities.

Management must recognise that because staff have their own agenda they must be fully engaged with the implementation of any plan and an incrementalist approach is adopted during implementation.

Each change is broken down into a series of smaller changes and management monitor how each small change has gone before implementing the next. This allows corrections to be made as required.

The foundational belief of the new modernist approach is that organisations have to be ready for whatever comes and be committed to dealing with it. This philosophy leads to the situation where chance events are seen as opportunities which the organisation can build on.

HOW TO USE IT

- Identify which planning paradigm your organisation favours *(see Theories 57 and 58)*.

- If your organisation has adopted Quinn's 'middle-of-the-road' approach then ensure you fully understand the long-term aims of the numerous incremental changes that you have to implement.

- Talk to frontline staff, customers, suppliers and competitors to stay abreast of what's 'bubbling under' in the marketplace *(see Theory 8)*.

- Use your knowledge of the intended incremental changes to plot a route that will make the journey easier for you and your staff.

- To deal with the 20% of truly unpredictable *(see Theory 81)* events train and develop your staff to show flexibility, spontaneity and creativity when reacting to customers' demands and changing market circumstances. Use simulations and role play for this.

- As you work with the organisation's planning process, identify any weaknesses and try to resolve them – while making sure you get the credit for your efforts.

- If you are in a position to choose a planning approach for your organisation then adopt the new modernism model as the best representation of reality. Even in today's world of change there are some things that we can predict with near 100% accuracy, such as England always losing on penalties to Germany.

QUESTIONS TO ASK

- How can I equip my staff to deal with uncertainty, change and the opportunities that they offer?

- To what extent are 80% of changes predictable and 20% unpredictable *(see Theory 81)* in my organisation?

THEORY 60

THE BOSTON CONSULTING GROUP MATRIX MODEL (CROWN AS KING)

Use to identify specific strategies you can use when considering the value of products and services to your organisation.

The Boston Consulting Group (BCG) created a matrix to assist organisations in deciding how to allocate investment among their products or services. By dividing the matrix into quadrants, four groups of products can be identified using as descriptors their position relative to market share and market growth rate.

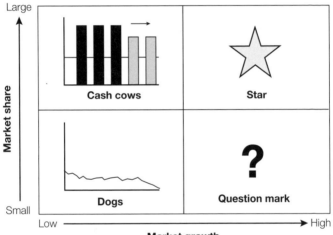

Source: Adapted from The BCG Portfolio Matrix from the Product Portfolio Matrix © 1970, the Boston Consulting Group.

When faced with the findings from a BCG matrix there are four possible strategies that organisations can adopt:

- **Build share:** Invest to increase market share, for example turning a question mark into a star or a dog into a cash cow.
- **Hold:** Invest just enough to keep the product in its present position.
- **Harvest:** Reduce the amount of investment in the product in order to maximise its short-term cash flows and profits.

■ **Divest:** Get rid of a product by selling or phasing it out. Question marks and dogs are the most likely to be sold off and the funds used to invest in question marks and stars.

HOW TO USE IT

■ Use the Pareto principle *(see Theory 81)* to identify the products and services that are the most and least profitable.

■ **Stars** are high-growth products or services competing in markets where they are relatively strong compared with the competition. Stars are the most important category because they are your future. You need to invest heavily in them to maintain their growth and maximise returns.

■ **Cash cows** consist of low-growth products or services with a relatively high market share. These are mature, successful products with relatively little need for investment. Milk your cash cows but also look after them and don't take them or their customers for granted.

■ **Question marks** are products or services with low market share but which operate in high-growth markets. They may have potential, but will require substantial investment in order to increase market share. It's with question marks that you really earn your money. You have to decide which to back and which to abandon.

■ **Dogs** refers to products that have a low relative share in a low-growth market. Dogs may generate enough cash to break even, but they are rarely worth investing in. If you work solely on a product which is classified as a dog then either get out or increase the product's market share. If you are responsible for deciding which products and units to keep you will have to decide which dogs to put down.

QUESTIONS TO ASK

■ Do I know which of my products are stars, cash cows, question marks and dogs?

■ Am I emotionally attached to a particular product or service, e.g. the first product I developed? Does my attachment cloud my judgement?

THEORY 61   # THE McKINSEY 7-S FRAMEWORK MODEL

Use this as a checklist to define and analyse the key dimensions in your organisation.

The 7-S framework was developed by Robert Waterman, Tom Peters and Julian Philips, whilst working at the McKinsey Group. The model suggests that the strength/well-being of any organisation can be described using seven interrelated elements. These are usually depicted as:

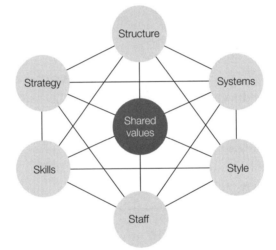

Source: van Assen, M., van den Berg, G. and Pietersma, P., *Key Management Models (2nd edn)* (Pearson Education, 2009).

Structure: The way the organisation's units relate to each other: centralised, functional divisions (top-down); decentralised; matrix; or network.

Systems: The procedures, processes and routines used to undertake important work. They include the systems for: finances, hiring, firing, promotion and performance appraisal systems and information systems etc.

Style: The cultural style of the organisation and how key managers behave in achieving the organisation's goals.

Staff: The numbers and types of personnel within the organisation.

Skills: The distinctive capabilities of individuals or of the organisation as a whole.

Strategy: A detailed plan for the allocation of a firm's scarce resources, over time, to reach identified goals.

Shared values: The interconnecting centre of McKinsey's model is shared values. This is what the organisation stands for and what it believes in. It's the organisation's central beliefs and attitudes.

HOW TO USE IT

- This is a complex model. Start by identifying what factors are contained in each element. Go into as much detail as you can. Use mind maps or lists for this *(see Theory 72)*. Your results will give you an invaluable insight into the many elements that are at play in your organisation.

- Study how the elements identified interact and react with the other elements. Some of the reactions may be quite subtle, others will be obvious. For example, introducing new systems will certainly affect skills, and may well affect structure, style and staff. It could even have an impact on strategy. Use a mind map to trace these connections.

- As in a game of chess, every move you make will change the relative strengths and weaknesses of every other piece on the board. It is these changes that you must identify and take account of.

- Your aim is to maximise and run with improvements and take action to minimise any weaknesses that your actions cause. You can only do this if you have an appreciation of how the elements interact with each other.

- Use on a daily basis to keep an eye on how the organisation is doing or use to predict/evaluate the impact that proposed changes may have on the organisation.

QUESTIONS TO ASK

- Do I know enough about the business to predict the effect that a change in one element will have on another?
- What can I do to gain even greater insights into the business?

THEORY 62 JOHNSON, SCHOLES AND WITTINGHAM'S STAKEHOLDER MAPPING THEORY

Use to identify the internal and external stakeholders that can affect your plans.

Gerry Johnson, Kevan Scholes and Richard Wittingham argue that mapping stakeholders is a strategic business tool which identifies and assesses the effect of different individuals or groups of stakeholders on the organisation *(see Theory 55).*

Stakeholders are recorded on a graph which plots their level of interest in issues that affect the organisation against the power they possess to exercise those interests. The stakeholders in this way are broadly divided into four groups:

High

Level of stakeholders' power

Don't take these stake-holders for granted but don't worry about them

Keep these stakeholders satisfied. They hold the key to the game

These stakeholders pose little threat in your plans, unless they gang up on you

These stakeholders may be important in the early stages so keep them informed about what's going on

Low   High

Level of stakeholders' interest

HOW TO USE IT

- Use in conjunction with Egan's shadow-side theory *(see Theory 55)*.
- Identify your stakeholders and their level of interest in the organisation.
- Identify those most likely to affect and be affected by your decisions.
- Use the above information to map and analyse the different groups of stakeholder according to their level of interest and power. Then set about making yourself known to them and winning their confidence. Talk to them and get to know how they feel about you and your work. Find out what's likely to motivate them to either support or oppose you and what they expect from you.
- Keep a watchful eye on those stakeholders with little power and little interest (the pawns) but don't waste too much time communicating with them.
- Talk to the ones with little power but high interest (the bishops). They may lack power to influence decisions but may be useful when it comes to working up the detail on your project or convincing other stakeholders.
- Put just enough effort into the ones with high power but little interest (the rooks) in order to keep them satisfied, but accept they may not want to get involved in the detail.
- Focus your attention on the ones with high power and high interest (the queens). These are the people you need to fully engage with to get the job done.
- Remember the more active you are as a manager, the more people you affect. It is like a game of chess where the more pieces you win or lose affects how well you do. The odd sacrifice may also have a major effect on whether you win or lose.

QUESTIONS TO ASK

- Do the key stakeholders even know that I exist?
- How am I going to raise my profile with all stakeholders?

THEORY 63 **PORTER'S VALUE CHAIN THEORY**

Use this to identify how you can improve organisational effectiveness by improving the quality of internal activities.

Michael Porter's value chain is a strategic business planning tool used to identify where competitive advantage arises in your business. It tracks the impact made on a product or service by every process from its start to delivery. The nine main stages of the value chain are grouped together as five primary activities and four support activities.

Primary activities	*Support activities*
Inbound logistics: Relationships with suppliers and activities required to receive, store and initially process inputs such as raw materials.	**Infrastructure:** Organisational hierarchy, strategic planning, financial and quality control systems.
Operations: The process of manufacturing or creating a product.	**HR management:** Recruitment, training and performance management.
Outbound logistics: Transportation, storage and distribution of product to the buyer.	**Technology development:** The hardware, software, procedures and technical knowledge involved in all operational processes.
Marketing and sales: Creating and analysing customer awareness of the product and supplying goods.	**Procurement:** Acquiring materials and all resources.
Service: Maintaining or updating and enhancing the product or service such as repairs or training after the product has been sold and delivered.	

Porter argues that competitive advantage can occur in any of the above activities.

HOW TO USE IT

■ Your level of knowledge about each of these stages will depend on your past experience and seniority. To fill gaps in your knowledge form a team that has representatives from each of the nine activities listed in the value chain.

■ Take each primary activity and identify which aspects of the activity create's value. Once you know where value lies, identify ways to maximise that value. But beware. Increases in one area may lead to decreases in another. For example, selling more products is great but if despatch can't handle the increased volume of traffic you may see a huge increase in complaints.

■ Review each support activity. Ask questions such as: Do human resources add value by recruiting the right people at the right time? Does IT provide the right training and equipment? If you are brave you may ask: Does senior management add value to the organisation? For reasons of survival you may want to answer '*yes*' in public.

■ Don't get bogged down in the detail. Look at the big picture and identify where the links are and how you can enhance each activity so as to maximise the value to you and your customers.

■ Remember the process can be applied organisation-wide or to just that part of the process which you manage.

QUESTIONS TO ASK

■ If I'm very familiar with one activity is there a risk that I may pay too much attention to it and not enough to the other eight?

■ How will other managers react to my review of their area of work? What can I do to get them onside before I start?

THEORY 64 PORTER'S FIVE FORCES THEORY

Use to summarise your current competitive situation.

Michael Porter's five forces theory is a framework for organisational analysis and business strategy development. Porter outlines five forces that determine competitive intensity and therefore the overall profitability of a service or product.

PORTER'S FIVE FORCES:

Threat of new entrants: Profitable markets that yield high returns will attract new entrants. This will eventually decrease profitability for all organisations in that sector.

Threat of substitute products or services: The existence of improved versions of your product and substitute, or near substitute, products increases the likelihood that customers will switch to alternatives – especially if they are cheaper or easier to access.

Bargaining power of customers: The ability of customers to apply pressure on the organisation, including resistance to price rises, increases when organisations supply a small number of big customers.

Bargaining power of suppliers: The ability of suppliers to charge excessive prices increases if there are a limited number of suppliers in the field.

Competition within the sector: For most organisations, the intensity of competitive rivalry is the major determinant of the competitiveness of the industry.

HOW TO USE IT

■ Look at each of the forces and analyse the strength of your current competitive position and identify the position you would like to be in *(see Theories 65 and 66)*.

■ How easy is it for customers to move suppliers? Keep one step ahead of your competition by improving what you offer or lowering prices to make substitution uneconomic. Aim to give your customers what they don't know they need by listening to your frontline staff *(see Section 8 and Theory 71)*.

■ Do you have a few very large customers? How easy would it be for them to drive your prices down? If you deal with a few powerful customers, they can dictate terms to you, and you need to broaden your customer base.

■ How easy is it for your suppliers to drive prices up? Can they hold you to ransom because they are sole suppliers of a product or service? Is it possible to switch suppliers? The fewer suppliers you have the more you are at their mercy. Find ways to broaden your supplier base. Start with the internet. Overseas suppliers are just a click away.

■ How strong are your competitors? If you have many competitors, and they offer equally attractive products and services, then your customers will move if the competition can provide a better/cheaper service. Keep a close watch on the quality of your products and services *(see Section 8)* and prices *(see Theory 74)* to make sure you maintain your competitive edge.

QUESTIONS TO ASK

■ When was the last time I methodically reviewed my team's competitive position?

■ How can I differentiate my products or services from those of my competitors?

THEORY 65 **SWOT ANALYSIS**

Use to summarise the strengths, weaknesses, opportunities and threats facing your organisation.

A SWOT analysis identifies the strengths, weaknesses, opportunities and threats facing your team or organisation. Strengths and weaknesses tend to emphasise internal factors while opportunities and threats concentrate on external matters. Often the same issue can be both a strength and a weakness or a threat and an opportunity.

All of the following examples can be seen as either:

Strengths and weaknesses	*Opportunities and threats*
Include: Current finances, customer loyalty, product range, employees' skills, the organisation's ability to react to changing circumstances, its relationship with stakeholders and the quality of management.	**Include:** Changes in competition, economic conditions, wider financial conditions, customer demographics, product range, declining/expanding market share, stakeholder relationships and technology.

Unfortunately 80% of all SWOT exercises are undermined by a lack of rigour. Too many contain overly optimistic statements about the organisation's current status and future prognosis. The worst offenders are senior managers who often see 'their' organisation through rose-tinted specs.

In addition, managers regularly fail to recognise that a strength is only a strength if it provides the organisation with a competitive advantage over its competitors. Good, committed staff are only a strength if your competitors have poor, uncommitted staff; while an opportunity only exists if the organisation has the commitment, resources and expertise required to take advantage of it.

HOW TO USE IT

■ First, define the focus of your analysis. What do you want to find out? What timescale do you want the analysis to cover? Remember, the further you try to look into the future the less accurate you'll be.

■ Once the objective is clear, select your group of participants. Choose six to eight people who have the experience, knowledge and skills to contribute to the process. Once selected don't allow the most senior person present to monopolise the meeting (even if that's you).

■ Make it clear to everyone that creativity must precede critical evaluation. If you become critical too soon people will clam up. So ban criticism in the early stages of the process. Out of the most bizarre utterances can crawl a great idea.

■ Brief the group as to the purpose of the meeting. Provide a list of headings that they might use to prompt discussion. Provide everyone with a supply of post-its on which to record their ideas.

■ Summarise the main points from the post-it and use this summary and your own notes from the meeting to compile a single list of ideas. Then take each suggestion and subject it to critical analysis – e.g. what evidence is there that the issue exists? If it does exist how can we measure its effect on the organisation? What's the likelihood of the event occurring and what would be its impact if it did happen?

■ Always examine opportunities for hidden threats and vice versa.

QUESTIONS TO ASK

■ How rigorous was the last SWOT exercise I ran?

■ Did I accept suggested SWOT without adequate evaluation?

■ Stick the post-it notes on the wall or board and group similar ideas together.

THEORY 66   **PEST/PESTLE ANALYSIS**

Use to analyse how the external environment impacts on your organisation.

The PEST process is forward-looking and is mainly concerned with the external environment in which the organisation exists. It tries to predict future political, economic, social and technological trends that may impact on the organisation in the future.

In recent years PEST has become PESTLE (PEST plus legal and environmental). Typically a PEST/PESTLE process would include consideration of the following examples:

ISSUES CONSIDERED IN A PEST/LE REVIEW:

Political, including changes in government following elections, financial and economic policies, legislation, health and safety regulations, employment law and European law/regulations.

Economic changes such as marketing data, predictions for economic growth, un/employment levels, conditions in the home, Euro Zone, world markets and banking policies.

Social trends, including an ageing population, changes in customer behaviour, impact of the web, social movements and changing social norms.

Technological trends, including government spending on research, new discoveries and developments, speed of technology transfer, impact of changes in information technology.

Legal issues, including changes in the law to employment, public liability, environmental, health and safety and working hours.

Environmental issues and changing public opinion concerning climate change, new energy sources and pressure groups.

HOW TO USE IT

■ Define the purpose of your PEST analysis. What do you want to find out? What timescale will the analysis cover? Remember the further you try to look into the future the less accurate you will be.

■ Once you've confirmed the terms of reference, select a group of 6–8 people from senior, mid and frontline staff *(see Theory 8)*. Those chosen must have a good knowledge of the organisation and the business sector it operates in and be capable of strategic thinking.

■ Because the group will contain middle and senior managers you must guard against one or two powerful personalities hijacking the meeting. If you think that their position might inhibit your actions appoint an outside facilitator to run the show – and brief them fully.

■ To avoid distractions hold the meeting away from work. Brief the group as to the purpose of the exercise and provide a list of headings that they can use as prompts. Provide everyone with a supply of post-it notes on which to record their ideas. At this stage suspend critical evaluation of even the daftest suggestion. Use the post-it notes and your own notes to compile a complete list of ideas.

■ When the list has been finalised assess each idea against the following criteria. How likely is it to happen? What impact will it have on the organisation if it does happen? What strategies and/or resources are required to minimise harm or maximise benefits should the event occur?

QUESTIONS TO ASK

■ How am I going to deal with any overly optimistic senior managers in the group?

■ How can I ensure that consideration is given to both quantitative and qualitative data during discussions *(see Theory 88)*.

THEORY 67 SCENARIO PLANNING

Use to identify possible futures for your organisation or team and plan for how to deal with them.

Scenario planning is as old as humankind. It involves asking the 'What will happen if?' question. Of course no one can predict the future but that hasn't stopped people trying.

Change does not progress in a nice straight line. It occurs in fits and starts. That means it's impossible to extrapolate what the future will look like based upon what happened today. In an attempt to get a handle on the future managers can use quantitative data (facts, figures, forecasts), qualitative data (people's opinions about what is going to happen) or a combination of both. Most commentators recommend that forecasts use a combination of quantitative and qualitative data and that a process similar to the following be used.

SCENARIO PLANNING PROCESS

DECIDE ON A TIME HORIZON FOR THE PLAN:
Identify the key issues and variables that will have the greatest influence on the company.
Agree a set of basic assumptions to be used in every scenario.
Develop alternative scenarios for all key variables and possible events.
List all combinations of the key variables.
Reject scenarios that are implausible.
Write up each of the remaining scenarios on a single side of paper.

HOW TO USE IT

- Gather together a small group of people to consider what might happen in the future. It's not a bad idea here to include a few science fiction/games fans in the group *(see Theories 65 and 66)*.

- Scenario planning is a time-consuming business; therefore focus on the key issues that are crucial to your team/organisation *(see Theories 60, 61, 63 and 81)*.

- Take each issue and follow the process outlined on the theory page. But do as all good chess players do and don't spend time looking at all possible scenarios for each issue. Instead concentrate on the 20% *(see Theory 81)* that will have the most significant impact on you/your organisation should they happen.

- Now that you have a manageable number of scenarios to work with evaluate each one fully. Use a mixture of quantitative and qualitative data in your analysis and forecasts *(see Theory 88)*.

- Remember that one very unlikely event, should it occur, can wipe you out. You must guard against such dangers. Toyota cars suffered a huge loss in production following the earthquake and tsunami in 2010. Toyota had planned for earthquakes but not for the effects of a tsunami.

QUESTIONS TO ASK

- How good am I at forecasting possible futures?
- How am I going to evaluate and rank the likelihood of each scenario occurring?

A FINAL WORD ON STRATEGIC MANAGEMENT THEORIES

WHY BOSTON CONSULTING GROUP WAS CROWNED AS KING

This was a difficult choice and several theories could have been crowned king. But then I remembered what Drucker said: 'There is only one valid definition of a business purpose – namely to create a customer.' Customers are created when they buy your products. Therefore the maintenance, growth and development of your product range is key to success. The BCG theory provides a strikingly clear way to analyse any product mix. If you know your business well you should have very little difficulty placing each product in the appropriate box and then using the advice provided by the model to decide what to do. A simple and ingenious theory.

Although I've crowned BCG as king I would offer one word of warning. Never refer to a product as a 'dog' within earshot of anyone who doesn't know what the term means. The Vice Chancellor and management team of one university decided to use the BCG grid to analyse the courses it offered. Somehow staff got wind of the fact that senior management thought that some courses were 'dogs' that needed to be taken out and shot. Within a day the email system was red hot as apoplectic academics fumed and students complained at the disparaging remarks.

You need to find out what role the organisation wants you to play in the planning process. Planning usually brings you into contact with a wide range of people in the organisation, some of whom may be able to assist you in your current work or future advancement. Either way, it's an opportunity to get noticed. Therefore, if your planning role is limited volunteer/negotiate to play a bigger part in the process – for the good of the organisation of course.

When drawing up or contributing to a strategic plan keep in mind the following:

- Planning is about the future and no one knows the future. Therefore any plan will be your best estimate. So avoid wasting time and energy in the search for perfection as all you'll get is spurious accuracy.

- Any strategic plan is a complex, interdependent document. Therefore, after every change review the whole plan for the knock-on effects that ripple through the plan.

- One weakness or threat can wipe out all the organisation's strengths and opportunities. Similarly, one strength can destroy all the weakness and threats faced by the organisation. You need to recognise such 'big beasts' for what they are when you find them.

- Contained within any threat there is an opportunity and within every opportunity a threat. Some computer manufacturers in the 1980s believed that there was no market for home computers and based their strategic plans on the continued expansion of the large mainframe market. Their actions turned an opportunity into a threat to their survival.

- If it can happen it will happen – given enough time. Therefore don't ignore any issue. Instead make a calculated judgement about how likely it is to happen and based upon that either include or exclude it from your plan.

Business is about competition and a SWOT or PEST/LE exercise can help you identify your competitive advantage. But don't fall into the trap of believing your own propaganda. Many high street banks like to claim that they have a loyal customer base (trapped) but I would argue that only First Direct Bank, with a 97–98% customer satisfaction rate, can claim loyal customers as a competitive advantage.

Finally, developing a strategic plan is not easy. The Chairman of my local football team decided to invest the club's money in building a new stand to enable the club to develop income flows from the advertising hoardings on the stand. As a fan first I thought he should invest in the team. Ten years on, and given the financial problems of so many football clubs, I have to admit he was right. But given that every strategic plan requires the support of numerous stakeholders I don't think that the Chairman did enough to win over people like me, or for that matter minimise the impact of our opposition to his plan.

SECTION 8

HOW TO MANAGE QUALITY

INTRODUCTION

According to Phil Crosby the study of quality has a lot in common with sex! Everyone wants more of it (under certain conditions); everyone believes they understand it (even if they can't explain it); everyone thinks they're good at it (another case of delusions of adequacy?); and of course we all believe that any problems are caused by other people.

It is difficult to have a meaningful discussion on sex, quality or any other complex subject until some basic assumptions are clarified. That is what this chapter is about. Read it and you will not only have a much better understanding of what quality is all about but also some useful ideas that you can apply. Alas I can't claim that it will improve your sex life!

Ask a group of people to name a quality product and the likelihood is that they will mention Rolex, Rolls Royce or Prada. This is because there is a tendency to measure quality in terms of price and prestige. The implications of this are that most people, unable to afford such luxuries, are deprived of quality. Yet there are many mid-price quality products available such as Tissot watches and Skoda cars (once the byword for junk on wheels). What we have to do is measure quality not in terms of price or prestige but relative to fitness for purpose; does the product or service do what we want it to do and is it accessible in terms of price and availability?

I chose 1980 as the starting point for theories in this section because; despite earlier work by many writers, it was in an interview with William Edwards Deming on NBC TV in 1980 that sparked off the so-called quality revolution. In the interview Deming was asked why America couldn't catch up with Japan in terms of manufacturing quality products. He warned the American public that he wasn't aware that Japan was waiting to be caught.

THEORY 68

DEMING'S SEVEN DEADLY DISEASES

Use this to diagnose the most likely disease that your organisation is suffering from.

The core of Deming's work is what he referred to as the Deadly Diseases that had infected western industry.

DEMING'S SEVEN DEADLY DISEASES ARE:

A lack of constancy of purpose, which creates organisations that have no long-range strategy for staying in business.

An emphasis on short-term profits, which undermines quality and productivity.

Evaluating performance by using merit rating or annual review systems, which nurture inter-organisation rivalry and destroys teamwork.

Mobility of management, which leads to a lack of understanding about the organisation and a reluctance to follow through on long-term objectives.

Running the organisation on visible figures alone, which fails to recognise the importance of unknown and unknowable figures such as the 'multiplier' effect of a happy customer.

Excessive medical costs for employee health care, which leads to an increase in the final cost of goods or services (he was writing about the USA).

Excessive warranty costs arising from customer dissatisfaction with goods or services.

Deming argued that the above could only be tackled by effective management that demonstrated a commitment to quality, communicated the quality message to staff and recognised the need to create a belief in total quality management throughout its workforce.

HOW TO USE IT

- To tackle the seven deadly diseases develop a plan for where you want be in 3–5 years' time *(see Section 7)*.

- Resist short-term thinking that might be advocated by others in the organisation. For example, reducing expenditure on training and development will boost profits in the short term. But where will that leave you three years down the line?

- Ask yourself, does our performance system reward outputs or outcomes? Outputs are what you produce, outcomes are how your customers feel about your product. There are many unknowable figures such as the 'multiplier' effect which occurs when a happy customer not only buys your product again but tells friends and family about it. Just because such figures are unknowable or can't be calculated doesn't mean you can ignore them.

- As for job-hopping managers, don't worry about them. Within every organisation there are a group of managers who are committed to the organisation. They are the middle managers who know that the grass isn't always greener elsewhere. They can deliver the organisation's long-term plans provided they are given the opportunity and not treated as dinosaurs by management.

- The final two diseases have been made worse by the litigious society which believes if there's blame there's a claim. Protect your staff, the organisation and yourself by eliminating the cause of legal claims and remove the causes of complaints by producing high-quality goods that are fit for purpose *(see Theory 69)*.

QUESTIONS TO ASK

- Is my organisation infected by one of the diseases?
- Do I see the cure as everyone's responsibility or restricted to the quality control team?

THEORY 69 **JURAN'S QUALITY TRILOGY**

Use to avoid losing customers because of poor quality.

Joe Juran is one of the founding fathers of Total Quality Management (TQM). He was an early proponent of benchmarking and quality costing and helped popularise the Pareto principle *(see Theory 81)*. He is best remembered for developing the quality trilogy which is composed of three managerial processes.

Quality planning identifies who the organisation's customers are and determines their needs. This information is then used to create processes that can produce the product or service that fully satisfies the customer's needs.

Quality improvement involves establishing the infrastructure needed for quality improvement. The first step is to identify the key 'production workers' and provide them with the resources, training and motivation required to be effective/successful.

Quality control measures quality performance against expectations, identifying where the gaps are and acting to rectify any deficiencies.

Juran considered that management were the cause of most quality-related problems. He cited their failure to identify the needs of customers *(see Theories 8 and 71)* and not having the right people and processes in place to meet these needs even when they are identified as the source of most quality problems *(see Theory 63)*.

HOW TO USE IT

■ Collect data on which activities cause problems, then analyse the activity to identify the root cause of the problem. It's uncanny how often Pareto's 80–20 rule applies *(see Theory 81)*. You will find that 80% of your quality-related problems can be attributed to around 20% of your organisation's activities.

■ Pull together a quality team (sometimes referred to as Forums or Circles) *(see Section 6)* that will drive your quality improvement programme forward. Choose people who are enthusiastic about improving quality.

■ Remember that although you may be the one who is the driving force behind the quality improvement project, quality is an organisation-wide issue and it's unlikely that you can tackle the problem without support from other managers. Build alliances *(see Theories 55 and 62)*.

■ Provide the team with the resources, training and skills they need to do the job *(see Section 4)*. Resourcing quality improvement programmes can be expensive but the alternative is a reputation for poor quality, lost orders and complaints.

■ Talk to your customers about what they expect from your products/ services. Are you meeting or, as Peters suggests, exceeding their expectations *(see Theory 71)*? If not, find out why?

■ Celebrate successes, no matter how small. The cumulative impact of many small improvements can be significant and will generate enthusiasm for further improvements *(see Theory 73)*.

QUESTIONS TO ASK

■ Have I got any quality champions within my team?

■ Have I built alliances with other managers across the organisation as a prelude to implementing a quality programme?

THEORY 70 CROSBY'S MATURITY GRID
(CROWN AS KING)

Use to understand the stages you and your team need to go through to establish a quality programme.

In *Quality is Free* Phil Crosby discussed the costs, in terms of warranty claims and poor public relations, to organisations of providing poor-quality goods. He argued that an organisation that established a quality programme would make savings that would more than cover the cost of any such programme.

Underpinning Crosby's belief was the principle of 'do it right the first time', which he felt was only achieved when an organisation reached a level of operational maturity. To achieve maturity organisations/individuals go through five stages.

Wisdom and certainty

Certainty: Knowing why you dont have a problem with quality.

Wisdom: Believing in the value of defect prevention as a part of all operations.

Enlightenment: Through good management and devoting sufficient resources to start resolving problems.

Awakening: Questioning if its necessary to always have problems with quality, but not willing to devote the resources required to address the problem.

Uncertainty: Not knowing why you have a problem with quality, thus creating a tendency to blame others.

Ignorance and uncertainty

Source: Adapted from Crosby, P. B., *Quality is Free: The Art of Making Quality Certain* (McGraw-Hill, 1978).

HOW TO USE IT

■ Build alliances with other managers who are interested in improving quality.

■ Take stock of where you are and get as many people as possible in your team/organisation to complete the Maturity Grid in *Quality is Free* or online.

■ Don't be surprised if the general view is that you are in the early stages of maturity. Moving from unconscious incompetence (doing things wrong and not knowing it) to conscious incompetence (still doing things wrong but knowing it) is the first step that you and your staff need to take. The second and third steps are to accept that most things don't work as they are supposed to and that problems breed problems. It is only when everyone accepts the reality of the situation that you can deal with the problem.

■ Before you can eradicate any problem it's essential that you accurately identify the cause of the problem *(see Theory 72)*. It only takes one bit of bad data to compromise the integrity of the whole procedure so check and verify all data as you receive it.

■ Don't rely on just statistical data in your analysis. Find out how people feel about the problem.

■ Only when you fully understand the problem, and have the resources to solve it, should you take action.

■ Define your customer's requirements, agree performance standards in advance and then let nothing stand in your way as you deliver them.

■ Once the new system is installed, monitor the level of complaints and adjust the system as required.

QUESTIONS TO ASK

■ Does my team see quality improvement as a significant issue?

■ Does my team see quality improvement as a one-off task or a continuous process?

THEORY 71 # PETERS, WATERMAN AND AUSTIN'S EXCELLENCE MODEL

Use this model to identify the features of an excellent organisation.

Tom Peters, Bob Waterman and Nancy Austin identified concern with the production of quality products as a fundamental feature of excellent companies.

THE EIGHT PREREQUISITES THAT ARE ESSENTIAL FOR MANAGING QUALITY ARE:

A bias for action: Encourage active decision making using cross-functional teams that include staff, customers and suppliers.

Staying close to the customer: An ability to identify what your customers want.

Autonomy and entrepreneurship: A willingness to foster innovation and nurture 'quality champions' throughout the organisation.

Productivity through people: A willingness to treat all employees as a source of quality and to respect, involve and empower them.

Hands-on, value-driven: Management should show its commitment to quality at all times and adopt a management philosophy that reflects this.

Stick to the knitting: Stay close to the business that the organisation knows about and has expertise in.

Simple form, lean staff: Develop simple organisational structures with a minimum of senior staff.

In 1985 Peters and Austin summarised their thinking on excellence as a concern for customers, a willingness to innovate, a well-motivated staff and a management and leadership consumed with a passion for excellence.

HOW TO USE IT

■ Listen to your customers. Get to know them and what they want. Be sensitive to their changing needs and seek to deliver what they want before they even ask for it.

■ Establish a cross-functional team with representatives from staff, customers and suppliers to examine how your service to customers can be improved.

■ Remember your customers may be internal or external.

■ Support innovation and enterprise in the organisation. Identify and nurture those people who have a passion for excellence and want to improve quality throughout the organisation.

■ See all employees as a potential source of quality and unlike the typical hard-nosed task-centred manager *(see Theories 12 and 13)* treat them with respect. Involve them in decision making and empower them to do their job. Do this and productivity and quality will improve.

■ Show your commitment to quality at all times and adopt a management philosophy that reflects this. Be a 'hands-on boss' not an 'absent landlord' *(see Theories 19–22)*.

■ To get the most from staff encourage them to use their discretion within clearly defined parameters. Provided they act in good faith never criticise staff for trying and failing *(see Section 3)*.

■ Stick to what you know best.

■ Keep organisational structures and systems simple. It's complexity that causes cock-ups.

QUESTIONS TO ASK

■ Who are my customers?

■ What are their true needs and expectations?

THEORY 72 ISHIKAWA'S FISHBONE MODEL

Use to analyse the cause and effect of problems.

Kaoru Ishikawa argues that it's important to explore all of the things that could cause a quality problem before you start to think about a solution. His fishbone model, developed in 1990, is a way of analysing cause and effect and can be summarised as follows:

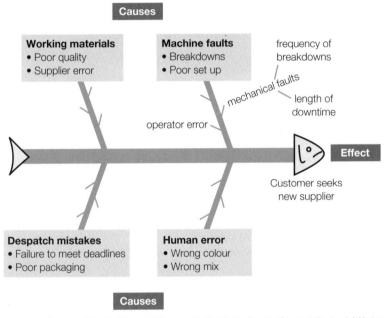

Source: Adapted from Ishikawa, K., *Guide to Quality Control (2nd edn)* (Asian Productivity Organisation, 1986).

The model is a bit like a mind map and is used to represent the problem and its causes diagrammatically. The difference with Ishikawa's model and more conventional mind maps is that the process is linear (better for logical thinkers).

HOW TO USE IT

■ Identify and define your problem. Write it in the box at the right-hand side of the page (you can draw the box as a fish's head if you are really keen on the symbolism). Then add the central spine of the fish.

■ Work out the major factors involved in the problem. Use brain storming to identify as many relevant factors as you and your team can think of *(see Theories 65 and 66)*. These factors are the 'large bones' running off the fish's spine (the ones you can choke on if you're not careful) (see diagram).

■ Analyse each problem ('big bone') and identify as many possible causes as possible. Connect these causes to the appropriate large bone as a series of 'medium-sized bones' (see diagram for start of analysis machine faults).

■ Analyse the results and investigate further. For complex causes you may have to attach 'small bones' to the medium-sized bones as your analysis of the problem delves deeper.

■ When complete don't sit back and admire your artwork – do whatever it takes to test and identify which of the possible causes is actually contributing to each problem. When you know what the real problem is identify and implement a workable solution.

■ The process isn't as complicated as it looks. Try it out on a work problem that you have already solved. I'll bet it throws up new factors that you didn't previously identify.

QUESTION TO ASK

■ Do I have the detailed knowledge required to identify the factors and sub-factors that might be causing the problem/s? If not, who can help me?

THEORY 73   IMAI'S KAIZEN 5S HOUSEKEEPING THEORY

Use this to appreciate the impact that very small-scale changes can have on quality.

Although Kaizen is a Japanese philosophy meaning change *(kai)* and to become good *(zen)*, it was the work of Masaaki Imai in the 1980s and 1990s that reinterpreted and popularised the philosophy in terms of management theory.

Imai suggests that Kaizen is a continuous improvement process that relies on teamwork, personal discipline, good morale, quality forums and suggestions for improvement. Much of what he has to say can be described as a plea for good housekeeping.

Tidiness (*seiri*)
Make sure the work place is free from clutter

Orderliness (*seiton*)
Arrange the equipment and materials you need
so that you can access them with ease

Cleanliness (*seiso*)
Ensure you clean and maintain equipment
on a regular basis

Standardising (*seiketsu*)
Make sure all equipment and processes
meet the required standard

Discipline (*shitsuke*)
Maintain what has been accomplished

Kaizen relies on incremental rather than abrupt change and the belief that all employees recognise that it's in their interests to produce high-quality goods and services. This is achieved by the elimination of waste and ineffi-ciency *(muda)* throughout the organisation.

HOW TO USE IT

■ Zen is all about simplicity and so is this theory. Read the theory again and you will see that there is nothing here that requires further advice from me. But just like Zen, to master the simple principles you need steely determination, self-discipline and consistency of purpose.

■ With Kaizen you must walk the talk and provide a role model for all your staff. After all, you can't demand that they keep their work areas tidy, and avoid accidents, if your office looks like a tip.

■ Remember, Kaizen is not about improving one aspect of your team's activity by 10%; it aims to improve each activity by 1%. The sum of these minor improvements will be huge in terms of quality and the pride your team takes in its work.

■ If you decide to adopt Kaizen start by doing a bit of management by walking about *(see Theory 10)*. Spend time on the shop floor or in reception to get an idea of how time, effort and resources are utilised. What you're looking for are small incremental improvements that you can implement easily and which will improve quality. You should also look out for good practices that you can spread across the organisation.

■ To help maintain the flow of ideas encourage staff to submit their ideas for improvements. Acknowledge and reward all suggestions made, even those you don't use.

QUESTIONS TO ASK

■ Do I have the self-discipline to implement Kaizen and continue the programme indefinitely?

■ How can I convince staff that by improving each activity by 1% the aggregate effect on quality will be huge?

THEORY 74 # THE BENCHMARKING MATRIX

Use this as a framework to identify internal and external best practices that you can use in your setting.

Benchmarking is a concept introduced by Frederick Taylor *(see Theory 3)* at the start of the twentieth century. He identified excellent performers by putting a chalk mark on their benches. This indicated to staff whose output or working practices they should emulate. This rather crude method of quality management has been refined over the past 100 years and is now a sophisticated tool used by many organisations.

	Product/Services	**Function/Processes**
Internal	A comparative analysis of the products and services produced or provided by different departments in the organisation	A comparative analysis of the functions and processes undertaken by different departments in the organisation
External	A comparative analysis of the products and services produced internally with those that exist in other organisations	A comparative analysis of the functions and processes undertaken in the organisation with those that exist in other organisations

Note: When undertaking external comparisons it is not necessary for the organisation to compare itself with other organisations in the same sector. For example, banks may learn a lot about the management of queues by comparing their practices with what goes on in supermarkets and fast food outlets.

HOW TO USE IT

- Key to any benchmarking process is understanding where you are on the journey to excellence *(use Theories 65, 66 and 70 to identify your position)*, and making sure that you go through the following four-stage cycle *(see Theory 49)*:

1 **The planning stage** is the most important and time-consuming activity in the model. Find out which subject areas are most important to your organisation. Which activities within each area need to be benchmarked? What's the best way to collect data on each activity? Who are the best practitioners of each activity?

2 **The doing stage** is where you start to experiment. Agree with your benchmarking partners the scope of the study and any ethical issues that may arise. Choose the most appropriate people to undertake the study and ensure that the organisation, at all levels, is committed to the project *(see Theories 55 and 62)*.

3 **The checking stage** is where you start to analyse the data and determine any gaps in quality. Use Ishikawa's fishbone model *(see Theory 72)* to identify the reasons for the gaps in performance and only then decide what action is required.

4 **The final stage** is where you take action. Involve everyone who has a stake in the changes, monitor the progress of the initiative and revise your strategy if necessary *(see Section 6)*. Use SMART targets *(see Theory 88)* to monitor progress.

QUESTIONS TO ASK

- How am I going to collect data from external organisations?
- Am I prepared to deal with all the findings from the exercise? What if pay or training levels are below best practice? Will the organisation be willing to invest in these areas?

THEORY 75 THE EXCELLENCE MODEL

Use this as a means of promoting awareness of, and action to improve, performance.

Malcolm Baldridge was the driving force behind the use of the Excellence Model as a means of promoting quality awareness in organisations. Baldridge's work was influential in America and it was the European Foundation for Quality Management (EFQM) that adapted and adopted his model for use in Europe.

The EFQM Excellence Model is underpinned by nine fundamental concepts that are divided into five enablers and four results:

- **The enablers** are the activities that the organisation must do well to be recognised as an excellent.

- **The results** are the measures used to assess the impact of the above activities.

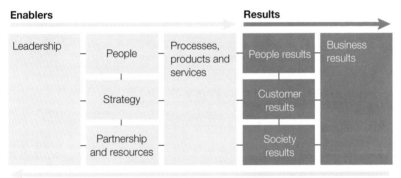

Source: Adapted from the European Foundation for Quality Management, copyright © EFQM 2012 Excellence Model, Brussels, Belgium, www.efqm.org

Although the EFQM does attach an award to the Excellence Model for organisations that want such recognition, application of the model is often used as a self-assessment tool for grading how an organisation is performing in each of the enabler and result areas.

HOW TO USE IT

■ Complete the online questionnaire available through the EFQM website. Grade your organisation/team against each of the nine categories. There are some helpful descriptors to help you grade each category.

■ If possible get a cross-section of your organisation/team to complete the questionnaire or better still everyone in your organisation.

■ Total up the scores and work out the average score across the organisation. Don't be alarmed if you only score 350 out of a possible 900. This is par for the course first time up. Of course 350 or less won't do in the long run. If you are a large organisation you may need to appoint someone to act as a quality champion. If you just did it for your team or department you may end up doing the entire job yourself.

■ Focus on the better scoring categories first to see if some quick wins can be achieved. Then work towards the categories where there is greater scope for improvement. Keep returning to the questionnaire and measuring what improvements have been made.

■ Remember, this is a self-assessment process; therefore your assumptions and impressions have to be tested. Get someone impartial to look at your assessment of what is going on and to challenge your analysis.

QUESTIONS TO ASK

■ Would going for the EFQM award motivate me and my team more than just using the process to improve performance?

■ Once the aims of the initial project have been met, how am I going to monitor, maintain and improve performance in the future?

A FINAL WORD ON QUALITY MANAGEMENT THEORIES

WHY CROSBY WAS CROWNED KING

As a fully paid-up member of the Deming Society (yes there really is such a body), crowning someone else as king is almost treason. But like all kingmakers sometimes you just have to do what's right. No one can doubt what Deming did to help restore Japan's industry. If his theories had the same quality as his practice there would be no competition. Sadly, they lack some of the appeal that Crosby's maturity grid has. Crosby's simple, but profound, insight that quality is free gives him the edge.

There is a lot of rubbish talked about quality management and plenty of so-called experts who are willing to blind you with management-speak and charge you for the privilege. About 20 years ago myself and a group of quality managers based in the West Midlands decided to rebel against the jargon and the influx of Japanese systems such as Kaizen, Kanban and Yoke Poke. We came up with the Black Country Quality Programme (BCQP), a programme specially designed for the needs of manufacturing companies in the Black Country. The programme included modules on:

■ *Yomaguddin* – refers to good practice as in 'You are a good one, old chap'."

■ *Weayobinthen* – refers to suppliers as in 'Why are you late, my good man?'

■ *Tayarfbostin* – refers to products/service as in 'Thank you, that's really very good'.

On 1 April we submitted the suite of modules to the government's Training Agency. Imagine the uproar when within days the Agency commissioned the programme! Maybe they were in on the joke.

The common thread that runs through most quality theories is the need for all stakeholders in the organisation to do everything possible to improve the quality of products, services and procedures in the organisation. This can be summed up by a desire to 'do things right first time every time'. To achieve this you must remember that quality improvement is an organisation-wide issue. It's not something that can survive long as a pocket of excellence in an otherwise hostile environment. So before you embark on a quality programme get all the senior managers on board first *(see Theory 55 and 62)*. Sell the programme by showing that the cost of doing things right first time is always less than the expense of trying to correct errors later.

Explore all of the causes of existing problems before you even start to think about a solution. As you begin, remember to go for small incremental improvements rather than massive abrupt changes. It's a lot easier to improve ten processes by 1% each than one process by 10%. Always celebrate your successes. This will motivate staff and help win over doubters. But don't just focus on short-term gains, think long term and with the help of frontline staff identify what your customers expect. Then work out how to exceed their expectations.

Use both internal and external comparisons of products/services and functions/processes as benchmarks and don't be shy about pinching good ideas wherever you find them.

Never fool yourself into believing that you are better than you really are. To avoid painting too rosy a picture, never base your calculations upon untested assumptions. Either independently verify the data or ditch it.

If you embark on a quality improvement programme you have to realise you are in it for the long haul. One managing director of a Black Country Engineering company told me how he spent over two years pushing TQM before he saw any real change in the staff attitude. 'But,' he said, 'I knew I had them when one morning they came in and switched on the machines before they put the kettle on.' On such signs is success built.

SECTION 9

HOW TO EXERCISE AUTHORITY, POWER AND INFLUENCE

INTRODUCTION

This is the shortest section in the book, containing just five theories. This is no reflection on how important an understanding of authority, power and influence is to managers. Rather, it is admission that this is a hugely complex and subtle area of study and that to do it justice would require an entire book. Rather than try and explain the intricacies of the three concepts I have chosen five theories which I think capture the essential points that you as a manager need to know.

All managers should be interested in exploring these three important and interrelated concepts. You need to know what authority, power and influence you have in the organisation you work for – not just in terms of your own staff and colleagues but also managers senior to you and the wider stakeholder community. Once you have a clear picture you can develop a strategy which will allow you to grow your authority, power and influence.

Many managers, especially those that have been newly promoted or appointed from outside the organisation, are reluctant to exercise their power and authority. Don't fall into this trap. As a manager you are given a certain level of authority and power and you are expected to use it. If you don't, you'll be written off by colleagues as someone who doesn't have the 'right stuff' to manage and be walked on by your staff.

The general advice given to military officers and teachers regarding the exercise of their power and authority is the same. Go in hard at first and make a statement about who is in charge. Of course, what is considered hard is context specific and I don't suggest that you have your staff double-timing around the car par park on your first day (maybe you could keep that for the second day). It's always easier to row back from this position once your feet are under the table than to go in too soft and then try to ratchet up your level of control. Remember you are a manager and your job is to get results, not to win popularity contests. Although this doesn't mean that you can't have a good relationship with your staff.

As for influence, it is perhaps one of the most under-rated tools available to a manager. Influence is to power what tai chi is to karate. Influence is soft and yielding, it bends in the wind and flows like water into areas that power can't reach. For example, a middle manager has no power over any director in the organisation but if they trust you and rate your advice you will have influence. This can come in very handy when you want their support for a project or when promotions are being handed out. Take every opportunity that arises to cultivate and extend your range of influence.

President Truman's advice to would-be leaders was 'walk softly and carry a big stick'. That's not bad advice for managers. What follows is an introduction to this fascinating area and I'd urge you to do some additional reading around the subject.

WEBER'S TRIPARTITE CLASSIFICATION OF AUTHORITY

Use to identify the different forms of authority that are available to you as a manager.

Max Weber identified three sources of authority or power. These were charismatic, traditional and legal-rational.

- **Charismatic** authority is defined by Weber as an 'extraordinary and personal gift of grace' (charisma) only given to a few. Staff are drawn to charismatic managers and believe that they are highly capable, have special abilities and can be trusted to deliver on their promises.
- **Traditional** authority or power is based on inheritance. It can be held by individuals, families, elites and groups and is passed from one generation to the next. For example, the power and status inherent in royal families is passed on through the line of succession.
- **Legal-rational** authority is the power that comes with a particular office. The office holder can exercise all the powers of that office until such time as they leave the post. For example, the Sales Director has the rational authority to direct all sales staff for as long as s/he holds that post.

The classic example of these three types of authority is taken from the Catholic Church. Christ, the head of the church, is charismatic. Catholic priests on ordination acquire traditional power over the laity and the Pope exercises legal-rational power over the entire church.

HOW TO USE IT

■ Identify the level of authority you have under each heading.

■ According to Weber charismatic authority is possessed by only a few. But, before you decide that you lack charisma revisit Theory 19.

■ Traditional authority is based on shared allegiance. If you are an outsider working in a family-owned business your opportunities for promotion to a senior position are limited unless you are willing to marry into the family. To fulfil your ambitions you may have to leave. But before you jump ship remember that traditional authority can exist in any organisation where the elite are united by shared histories of public school, university, the military or any one of 100 other experiences.

■ As a manager, you automatically have some legal rational authority and people expect you to use it. Don't disappoint them.

■ Typically most readers of this book will have little or no traditional power, some charismatic power and, depending on your seniority, a significant amount of legal-rational power.

■ Work on increasing your charismatic power *(see Theory 19)*.

■ Identify the extent of your legal-rational power and be willing to use it. Too often managers fail to use the power they have because they are embarrassed telling people what to do *(see Theory 11)*. Away with such conceits. Management is hard enough without you refusing to use all the tools available to you.

QUESTIONS TO ASK

■ What are the limits of my legal-rational power?

■ What elements of charismatic power (honesty, integrity, loyalty) do I possess?

THEORY 77 FRENCH AND RAVEN'S SOURCES OF POWER THEORY (CROWN AS KING)

Use to understand how to exert influence on an interview panel, your boss or your staff.

There are numerous models of power. One of the most compelling was outlined by French and Raven in 1959. They identified five sources of power that a person, real or corporate, can call upon to encourage or compel compliance.

Legitimate: Where the person's position carries with it a reasonable expectation that staff will follow their directions.

Reward: The capacity to grant or withhold financial and non-financial rewards to people.

Coercive: The capacity to impose sanctions or punishments on another person or group.

Expert: Where an individual's expertise in a particular area means that others are willing to follow their advice/instructions. This power only exists for as long as that person's expertise is required.

Charismatic: The ability to command compliance by example or force of personality.

Of the five power sources French and Raven suggest that charismatic power is the most significant as its holder can influence people over time and distance *(see Theory 19)*. It is the Holy Grail of leadership. It accounts for why millions of black Americans, who had never met Martin Luther King Jr, were willing to march and risk injury and even death to follow his example of peaceful protest.

HOW TO USE IT

- As a manager you hold a position of authority. Identify the limits of that authority. Act with confidence when you exercise authority and expect staff to comply *(see Theory 11)* with your legitimate requests. Expect compliance and enforce it.

- Identify the range of rewards you can offer staff and remember they need not be financial. Public recognition or a new desk may mean more to a person than promotion or a pay rise *(see Theory 17)*. Always deliver on any promises you make.

- Identify the limits of your coercive power. Never use coercive power to bully people but it is perfectly legitimate to pick up on poor performance and apply a suitable sanction. Staff are often unaware that they are under-performing. An unofficial chat can often negate the need for more formal action.

- Identify what, if any, expert power you have. If you have a professional qualification you have a degree of expert power. Gain specialist knowledge in one or more hot areas of your discipline and use it in your organisation.

- Alas, few of us can match the charisma of your average Hollywood superstar. But charisma is in the eye of the beholder. So think about how you appear to your staff. Act with confidence and integrity and provide them with a vision they can buy into *(see Theories 19–22)* and they will think you have charisma, just not as much as a superstar!

- Accumulate as many sources of power as possible because when two or more sources are combined synergy occurs. A case of $2 + 2 = 5$.

QUESTIONS TO ASK

- What sources of power do you have access to?
- Who in your organisation exercises power? What can you learn from them?

THEORY 78 SOURCES OF INFLUENCE

Use to analyse the constituent parts of the quality problem you face.

Influence differs from power in that it seeks to persuade, not compel, people to comply with your requests. With power you can force people to follow your orders, but it's not a recipe for a happy team. Managers need to master the softer arts of influence and persuasion.

Writers, psychologists and management gurus have identified various sources of influence or strategies that managers can use. Below are seven that appear in many lists.

SOURCES OF INFLUENCE INCLUDE:

Let people believe that you are just like them. People respond more positively to those they think share their views and beliefs.

Make people feel comfortable. Use active listening – repeating back to the person things they have said demonstrates that you are listening.

Find out what motivates the person and supply it.

Allow the person to play some part in any decision-making process that affects them – even if it's only minor.

Highlight how special and unique the offer is that you are making to the person.

Remember the value of reciprocity and exchange favours.

People are impressed by displays of expert knowledge so find ways to demonstrate your knowledge, without showing off.

HOW TO USE IT (1) – INFLUENCING AN INTERVIEW PANEL

■ First impressions count. In order to survive our ancestors had to make instantaneous judgements about strangers they came across in a jungle clearing. The only information our ancestors had was how the person looked. The more like them the safer they felt. That trait has stayed with us. Interviews are won and lost in the first 90 seconds. Find out the organisation's dress code in advance and arrive suitably dressed.

■ Find out what the organisation is looking for. Check the advert, job description, person specification, website and talk to anyone you know who works there. Having identified the traits and skills required demonstrate them in the interview and the rest of the selection process *(see Theory 11)*.

■ If you look uncomfortable and nervous the panel will pick up on it. Relax and smile (but not like a deranged serial killer) and be approachable. Remember, it's how you are perceived that's important not how you feel *(see Theory 11)*.

■ People want what they can't have. Think of the interview as a first date. Put your best attributes on show, but make it clear that you possess other assets as well. Convince the panel that your unique talents won't be found in any other candidate.

■ People are impressed by expert knowledge especially when it's unexpected. The best way to demonstrate this is to do your homework about the organisation and ask one or two searching questions about its operations.

QUESTIONS TO ASK

■ Who is going to be on the interview panel? What can I find out about them from friends, contacts or via the internet/social media?

■ Based on what I know about the interviewers, what characteristics should I emphasis/minimise?

HOW TO USE IT (2) – INFLUENCING YOUR BOSS

■ You can also use the sources of influence listed above with your boss. But you need to change your tactics and remember that they may know more about power and influence than you do. So be subtle.

■ Don't try and imitate your boss, it will only annoy them.

■ Your boss will value specific jobs or functions that you perform more highly than others. Find out which these are and make sure you deliver them to a high standard

■ Don't present your boss with a major change or initiative out of the blue. Keep them informed about anything you are working on, ask their advice – even if you don't need it – and keep them in the loop.

■ Become invaluable to your boss. Often senior managers don't like getting involved in the detail. Identify an area of work that your boss is weak in and become the house expert on that issue. Brief your manager in a language they understand but never let on that you know more than they do.

■ Be willing to exchange favours with your boss but don't let this become a one-way route. If they want something make sure you get something in return. No one likes a lickspittle.

■ Listen to your boss even if they bore you about their wonderful shot to the fifteenth green. People like people who are interested in them.

■ Be willing to take on any good ideas and suggestions made by your boss but critically evaluate each idea. If you need to challenge their proposals present your objections, in private, as a series of alternative approaches for discussion rather than a direct challenge.

QUESTIONS TO ASK

■ What beliefs, common experiences, interests or traits do you share with your boss? How can you use these to your advantage?

■ What traits in staff does your boss most admire/look for?

HOW TO USE IT (3) – INFLUENCING YOUR STAFF

■ If you use power to compel your team to complete a task they will say that 'The boss made us do it'; if you use influence they will say 'We did it'. Only use power if influence fails.

■ Lay the groundwork for using influence by establishing good working relationships with your staff.

■ Identify those things that you have in common with your staff. These may be a love of football or films, brought up in the same area, went to similar schools, shared training experiences etc.

■ Show an interest in the opinions and views of staff and praise their insights.

■ Let staff play some part in any decision-making process that affects them, even if this just involves leading them through the decision-making process that you followed and asking them for their opinions at each stage.

■ You should know what motivates your staff *(see Section 3)*. Use this knowledge to present your case in the form that will be most attractive to them.

■ Explain how important their acceptance of the idea is to you and how special and unique the offer is that you are making to them.

■ Use any status that you have as an expert to sway their thinking.

■ Remember you will achieve greater success if you offer the person a win–win solution *(see Theory 9)* and there is nothing unethical in using a bit of transactional leadership to get someone onside *(see Theory 17)* or creating an in-group you can rely on for support *(see Theory 18)*.

QUESTIONS TO ASK

■ What leverage/approach can I use with each member of staff?

■ Are there specific individuals whom I need to get on board?

THEORY 79 # MACHIAVELLI'S GUIDE TO SURVIVAL

Use to protect yourself against Machiavellian colleagues and bosses.

Out of work and looking for a job Machiavelli penned a job application to the Magnificent Lorenzo de Medici. In the history of the world it was one of the better job applications and was later published as *The Prince*.

MACHIAVELLI'S SURVIVAL GUIDE FOR LEADERS PROVIDES A WIDE RANGE OF ADVICE INCLUDING:

Leaders must deal with the reality that confronts them not the reality they wish existed.

Leaders must never rest on their laurels. Instead they should use quiet periods to plan their future strategy.

It's safer to trust an old enemy than an old friend because the enemy will be grateful and constantly seek to demonstrate their loyalty.

An act is virtuous if it achieves its aim – a case of the ends justifying the means.

To avoid future conflict a new leader must destroy the remnants of the old regime completely.

Those who help a leader achieve power often become a threat because they believe that the leader is indebted to them. They must be eliminated.

Leaders should eliminate any threat to their position before it has a chance to grow.

It's better for a leader to be feared than loved as the fear of retribution buys more loyalty than love ever can.

HOW TO USE IT

■ In applying this entry I don't suggest that you buy a white Persian cat which you stroke languidly while interrogating your staff. Rather, use Machiavelli's ideas as a defence against conspirators, psychopaths and Machiavellian bosses and colleagues.

■ As a manager never fool yourself, or allow anyone else to mislead you, about the reality of the situation you face. Only by confronting reality can you deal with the present and plan for the future.

■ Never rest on your laurels. Use down-time to search for potential threats and opportunities and devise a strategy for dealing with them should they occur *(see Theories 65–66)*.

■ As an employee protect yourself against managers who believe that the ends justify the means. They are unlikely to shy away from disposing of you if it suits their purpose. Remember it's better to be useful to a Machiavellian manager than to be their friend.

■ Many new senior managers change their management team within a year of appointment as a way of stamping their authority on the organisation and staff. If you think this may happen prepare an escape route just in case you need it.

■ Anyone you helped reach a position of authority may see you as a threat. If this is a possibility make yourself useful to them or plan your escape.

■ Avoid investing your work with too much emotional significance (feeling of belonging, status, worth). Corporate organisations have no such feelings. Their contract with you is based on a business transaction and if they need to let you go they will. Recognise this and rethink your relationship with work and you will never be disappointed or surprised by how you are treated.

QUESTIONS TO ASK

■ How can I recognise a Machiavellian manager?

■ What's my strategy for dealing with Machiavellian managers?

THEORY 80   RONSON'S PSYCHOPATH TEST

Jon Ronson, in his 2011 best-seller *The Psychopath Test: A Journey through the Madness Industry*, suggests that most organisations contain one or two psychopaths and that they can do untold harm if they are not identified and dealt with. He lists 20 traits that are characteristic of psychopathic behaviour. The eight most easily observed traits in psychopathic managers are detailed below.

TRAITS OF THE WORKPLACE PSYCHOPATH INCLUDE:

Glibness and superficial charm.

An inflated sense of self-worth.

Compulsive and pathological lying.

Cunning and manipulative behaviour.

Lack of guilt, remorse or feelings for others.

Easily bored with poor impulse control.

Impulsive and risk taking.

Irresponsible.

Unfortunately, several of these skills are very useful in interviews and socially aware psychopaths are regularly appointed and promoted to management posts. Therefore managers need a strategy for dealing with such people.

HOW TO USE IT

■ When dealing with a psychopath, follow the old boxing maxim and defend yourself at all times.

■ If you are concerned about someone's behaviour raise your concerns with HR and get them recorded. Don't call the person a psychopath – you're not qualified to make such a diagnosis – simply describe in detail the behaviour you have observed or been subject to.

■ Maintain meticulous records of your dealing with the person. Psychopaths are great liars and will distort past events and conversations and claim your successes as their own if it suits their aims.

■ Protect your staff by monitoring their dealings with the person and keep a note of any outcomes or decisions. Remember these people have no conscience and will skewer anyone who gets in their way.

■ Develop good relationships with staff and other managers. That way if the person does make malicious allegations against you numerous people will be ready to question the claims made because they won't chime with what they know about you.

■ When dealing with the person follow the organisation's policies and procedures to the letter, especially if they are a member of your staff. The corporate psychopaths of this world aren't above claiming harassment of some kind if it helps their cause.

■ Deprive the person of any grounds for attack. Develop your reputation for integrity *(see Theories 19–22)* and walk the talk. If it comes down to someone's word, who do you think staff and management are going to believe, you or them?

QUESTIONS TO ASK

■ Does anyone I work with exhibit the traits listed in the theory?

■ What is my strategy for dealing with them?

A FINAL WORD ON AUTHORITY, POWER AND INFLUENCE THEORIES

WHY FRENCH AND RAVENS WERE CROWNED AS KINGS

Other writers have examined the sources of power and produced much longer tracts on the subject. They have examined the nature of power, how you get hold of it, how you keep it and how it can be lost. But none have been as succinct as French and Ravens or identified so clearly how synergy occurs when you can access power from a variety of sources. The identification of synergy more than any other factor makes this theory a worthy recipient of the title of king.

Many years ago I read something which said unless you have experience of managing staff before you're 27 you'll never make a good manager. Over the years I've mulled this idea over and come to the conclusion that the writer had been on to something but had reached the wrong conclusion.

In everyday situations most British people are fairly diffident. They don't like telling other people what to do or barking orders. They are terrified that if they do tell someone what to do the other person will turn around and say 'Who put you in charge?' Such a retort would be very embarrassing, and as we all know social embarrassment is worse than physical injury to most British people. So people hesitate to take control and as time passes the harder it becomes for them to throw off their learned behaviour and tell someone what to do.

But if you're a manager you can't be diffident. You are paid to take control regardless of how you are feeling. Therefore you have to tell people what to do, even if that means challenging years of learned behaviour and socialisation. When you become a manager you are given a certain level of traditional and legitimate authority and both your employers and your staff expect you to use it. So don't disappoint them. Authority is there to be used – so exercise it.

Work to accumulate as many sources of power as possible. Typically some degree of legitimate reward and coercive power come with the job of manager. You need to test the limits of each and build up your expert power. As for charismatic power, that's something we all need to work on (see Theory 19).

In terms of influence, the first thing you need to do is sell yourself to your boss and you're staff. One sure way to achieve this is to support both of them in public and only raise doubts, concerns or criticisms in private. Both parties will appreciate this.

When attending an interview remember that the panel want to appoint someone. They aren't seeing six or more people because they enjoy meeting new people. They have a post to fill and they clearly hope that you will be the one to fill it. So treat the interview as a meeting of equals and present the best possible version of you that you can.

When dealing with a Machiavellian boss remember that they are logical people who operate in their own self-interest. Your best defence against any attack is to find ways to be useful to them. As long as you remain useful they will be happy to keep you on.

Psychopaths can be male, female, your boss, colleague or member of staff. The only difference between them will be the tactics they use to get their way. One or two of them exist in every organisation. Whatever position they fill, keep detailed and accurate records of all your dealings with them and if necessary make your concerns known to HR. Violent psychopaths are very rare but the common or garden variety that you might encounter at work can destroy your life and career with false accusations and malicious rumours so defend yourself at all times and have as little to do with them as possible.

SECTION 10

THE BEST OF THE REST – A MISCELLANY OF GREAT IDEAS FOR MANAGERS

INTRODUCTION

This section contains nine great theories each of which could have been squeezed into one of the other sections. But I wanted to end with a selection of theories that transcend neat classification. Why? Because management transcends neat classification. For example, there are nine theories of motivation discussed in this book. Does that mean that as a manager you can only motivate staff when you use one of those theories? Of course not. Your personality and style of management, how you talk to people and take account of their needs when planning or managing change all impact on their motivational levels. This section is intended to remind you that the knowledge gained from one theory can often be applied in numerous situations, so don't build arbitrary walls between theories.

The Pareto Principle, which kicks off this section, is a great example of how one theory can be applied in numerous situations and help managers identify where they should concentrate their efforts. Others, such as the Eisenhower principle, will help you identify what tasks you should be doing and which you should either bin or delegate, and some provide insights into your personality and the personalities of those you work with.

There is even a bit on Neuro Linguistic Programming thrown in for good measure. When I told a colleague that I'd reduced NLP theory to 200 words they said I was mad. But I'll leave you to decide. Salvador Dali asked critics not to admire him for the method in his madness but for the madness in his method. When I took on the challenge of reducing great ideas to around 250 words it felt at times like madness, It's impossible to capture everything about NLP or the other great ideas, all I can do is whet your appetite to read more about them.

I hope you enjoy reading this section but don't look for or expect to find a single theme to emerge as you read 'cos there ain't one.

THEORY 81 | # THE PARETO PRINCIPLE (CROWN AS KING)

Use Pareto to identify where you need to concentrate your efforts to maximise your results.

The Pareto principle is possibly the single most useful theory that a manager can know about. Why? Because it can be used to reduce significantly a manager's workload and is applicable in a huge range of circumstances.

The principle was devised by the Italian economist Vilfredo Pareto. He first used it to demonstrate that 80% of the wealth in Italy was owned by 20% of the population. Joseph Juran, the quality guru *(see Theory 69)*, stumbled across his work and helped to popularise its use.

It was quickly found that the 80/20 split could be applied to a vast array of social and business situations. For example 80% of an organisation's sales are made to 20% of its customers.

This theory of 'the vital few and the trivial many' does not pretend to be a precise measure of any phenomenon. The split may be 70/30 or 90/10. It's a rule of thumb which can be applied to a wide range of questions relating to staff, products, resources, customers and suppliers but the precise split will differ from instance to instance.

HOW TO USE IT

The following are just a few examples of how you might use the Pareto principle.

- 20% of your staff will cause 80% of your staffing problems. Sort out the 20% and leave the others alone.
- 20% of your staff contribute 80% of your productivity/profits/sales etc. Reward them!
- 20% of your customers generate 80% of your sales. Make sure you look after your golden egg laying customers.
- 20% of your debtors owe 80% of debts outstanding. Concentrate collection efforts on these people.
- 80% of complaints originate with 20% of customers. Identify why there is a problem with these particular customers and tackle it *(see Section 8)*. Usually you will be able to resolve the problem but many years ago I simply refused to supply one customer because of his unreasonable demands which meant that we lost time and money on his orders. Customers are usually right but some are not worth the hassle.
- 80% of expenses incurred by the organisation will be in 20% of the budget headings. It is these big cost centres that you need to keep under close observation and where you should look for savings.
- 80% of your income will be earned from 20% of your products *(see Theory 60)*. You need to guard against over-reliance on a small number of products. Your future survival depends on it.

QUESTION TO ASK

- Which three areas can I use this theory on immediately?
- Which 20% of the jobs I do add most value?

THEORY 82   THE EISENHOWER PRINCIPLE

Use to prioritise your workload and manage your time more effectively.

The Eisenhower principle describes how President Dwight D. Eisenhower organised his workload. Eisenhower's insight was that you should throw away all those to-do lists that you laboriously update each day and instead concentrate on doing what's important to you. By definition, only work that helps you achieve your aims is important. Bearing in mind that he masterminded Operation Overlord (D-Day), he probably knew what he was talking about.

One theory suggests that you divide tasks into four groups.

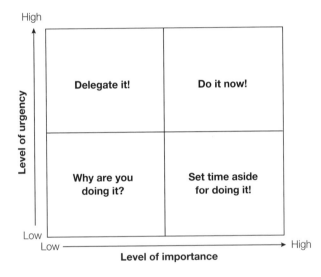

HOW TO USE IT

- Get rid of your to-do lists. Instead list the work that helps you achieve your aims. This includes keeping your boss satisfied. You also need to keep your manager's boss happy as it is they who will appoint your manager's successor.
- Once you have your list of work allocate it to one of the following four categories.

  1 Why are you doing this? If it requires action delegate it – if not bin it.

  2 Delegate it! Don't let someone else's crisis become your urgent problem. By all means help colleagues but make sure that their work is slotted into your priorities. Be assertive. Avoid time thieves. They steal a commodity which once lost you can never recover.

  3 Set time aside for doing it! The place won't fall apart if you don't do these things now. But don't keep putting them off or else they may come back to bite you.

  4 Do it now! These are probably the issues that you currently spend most time on. They need to be dealt with quickly and they help you achieve your aims.

  5 To reduce the number of do-it-now jobs landing on your desk tackle some of the set-aside tasks languishing in your drawer. If you can sort these out you will eliminate the source of many problems. For example, tackle the source of customer complaints and urgent complaints will reduce *(see Section 8)*. You can never eliminate all the do-it-now items but good forward planning can reduce the amount of time you spend buzzing around like a blue-a**** fly.

QUESTIONS TO ASK

- If tackled, which of the set time aside jobs in my in-tray would save me most time?
- Which tasks should I redirect at source to another member of staff so that they never reach my desk?

THEORY 83 **THOMAS AND KILMANN'S CONFLICT RESOLUTION MODEL**

Use to understand and deal with conflict in your team.

Kenneth Thomas and Ralph Kilmann identified five approaches for resolving conflict. Each approach is described according to the level of assertiveness and cooperativeness displayed by the parties involved in the conflict.

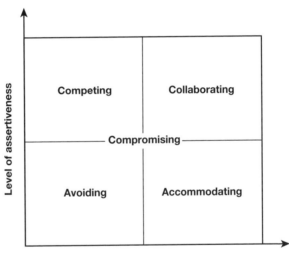

Source: Adapted from 'Conflict and Conflict Management' by Kenneth Thomas in *Handbook of Industrial and Organizational Psychology*, edited by Marvin D. Dunnette, p. 900, 1976. Adapted with permission.

Collaborating requires high assertiveness and high co-operation from all parties. This approach tries to fully satisfy everyone.

Accommodating involves low assertiveness and high co-operation. This approach indicates a willingness for one party to satisfy the needs of others at the expense of their own.

Compromising involves moderate assertiveness and co-operation and tries to ensure that all parties are at least partially satisfied.

Competing leads to high assertiveness and low co-operation and is designed to ensure that one person wins at the expense of everyone else.

Avoiding involves low assertiveness and low co-operation and is designed to avoid conflict and means that no party is satisfied.

Thomas and Kilmann argue that once a person understands the categories they can select the most appropriate approach to take in each new situation.

HOW TO USE IT

- Conflict and disagreement are rife in the workplace. So how do we avoid it? That's the first trap. Don't try to avoid conflict, instead resolve it. If you resolve conflicts as they arise you eliminate future causes of conflict.

- Start by identifying your default position – your instinctive reaction to conflict. There isn't a questionnaire to help you do this. So think about how you dealt with a couple of recent conflict situations. Be honest in your assessment of your default position

- Knowing your default position, approach each new situation in a calm and respectful manner. Be courteous with the other person(s) and listen carefully to what they have to say (see Theory 9). Try to separate the problem from the person(s). Just because they hold a different position to you doesn't mean that they are aggressive or negative.

- Set out the facts and settle on some points that you can both agree on. Then explore the various options available to you. Set some goals and deadlines that you can both agree on and start to work towards them. As you make progress, mutual trust and understanding will develop between you. This will make it possible to tackle any outstanding problems that you still have.

- Even among friends legitimate differences of opinions can escalate into full-blown arguments and major fall-outs. To avoid this, remain non-confrontational and focus on the issue not the person.

QUESTIONS TO ASK

- When faced with conflict am I too weak or aggressive?
- Do I need assertiveness or anger management training?

THEORY 84 GRINDER AND BANDLER'S NEURO LINGUISTIC PROGRAMMING (NLP) FILTERING THEORY

Use to remind you that what you say (transmit) is not always what is heard (received).

John Grinder and Richard Bandler suggest that our brain's perception of events may be different from reality. This action is described as a filtering process that helps us to create the interpretations upon which we base our actions.

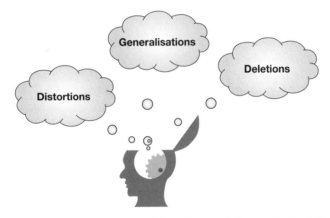

There are three filters (Deletion, Distortion and Generalisation) that are important because:

Deletion prevents our brain from having to absorb the mass of sensory information that we are exposed to every second and removes information that we consider irrelevant.

Distortion allows us to fit an event or occurrence into a framework of pre-existing knowledge. It changes our interpretation of events to fit our existing understanding.

Generalisation enables us make a judgement based on something similar that we may have experienced previously.

HOW TO USE IT

■ Using communication techniques such as NLP depends on building a rapport with the other person. Start by finding common ground and then maintain a good rapport through effective use of language, gestures and tone *(see Theory 31)*.

■ One of the key pillars of NLP is the belief that the meaning of your communication is determined by the response you get and not what you meant. Therefore take great care in how you frame each communication.

■ Decide on what it is you want the other person to do as a result of the communication. This is the outcome you want.

■ Put your message over as clearly, accurately and unambiguously as you can.

■ Use verbal and non-verbal communication, e.g. body language, to emphasise particular points.

■ Look for clues that indicate whether or not the person understands what you are trying to communicate.

■ Use the feedback you get to identify if they are deleting, distorting or over-generalising the information you have communicated to them. Correct such misunderstandings during the conversation.

■ If at first you don't get the response you wanted try a different approach.

QUESTIONS TO ASK

■ Do I listen actively to what my staff say?

■ Do I seek to be understood not just heard?

THEORY 85 GOLEMAN'S THEORY OF EMOTIONAL INTELLIGENCE

Use this to become a better manager by increasing your self-awareness and understanding of others.

Daniel Goleman's work in the 1990s on emotional intelligence (EI) popularised the idea that it is not sufficient for managers to have a high IQ and be technically skilled. If they wanted to win the hearts and minds of staff they also needed to be emotionally intelligent. Goleman identified five characteristics that managers needed to develop if they were to be successful. These are:

Self-awareness: Managers must recognise their own emotional states and the impact their emotions can have on others.

Empathy: Managers need to identify with and understand other people's feelings when making decisions.

Self-regulation: Managers must control their emotions and impulses and be able to adapt to changing circumstances.

Social skills: Managers need to manage relationships, influence people and encourage them to move in the direction that they have identified.

Motivation: Managers must develop their own source of intrinsic motivation. They can't rely on external rewards to motivate them. Achievement of their goals will provide the ultimate satisfaction *(see Section 3)*.

Goleman believes that possessing self-awareness and an understanding of others can make an individual both a better person and a better manager.

HOW TO USE IT

- Establish your Emotional Intelligence Quotient by completing one of the many online questionnaires that are available. Self-awareness is critical so be honest when you go through this process.

- Keep a reflective diary. This doesn't have to be of Pepysesque proportions. Just jot down any key incidents that took place during the day: what you did, why you did it, what impact it had on you and on others. You can then review it and consider how you could have done things differently/better.

- Try to look at situations from other people's perspectives. This doesn't mean you must follow their line or even agree with what they have to say. However, by trying to be empathetic and recognising that people are entitled to their views and beliefs you will lay the foundations for effective dialogue.

- Take time to listen attentively to the other person's viewpoint and control the urge to jump in and make rushed or emotional decisions; and never start a sentence with 'If I were you ...' – 'cos you ain't.

- There will be times when you feel you can't compromise. This may be down to your own principles and beliefs. Recognise that other people may also have deep convictions about an issue. Don't allow yourself to become frustrated or angry if they also refuse to compromise. Stay calm and re-examine your values in the light of what they have to say and seek to find a solution that is acceptable to both of you.

QUESTIONS TO ASK

- Do I believe that having a high EI is important in the workplace?
- If I think it is important, how much do I really know about it/use it?

THEORY 86 BOYD'S OODA LOOP

Use to enhance your decision-making skills.

John Boyd was a US Air Force Colonel who developed the OODA model as a decision-making tool in air combat. The model was quickly picked up by managers in other sectors.

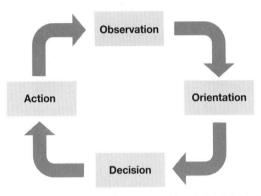

Source: Adapted from Clayton, M., *Management Models Pocket Book* (Management Pocket Book, 2009).

Observation: Collect up-to-date data from as many sources as possible. But remember that all decisions are based on incomplete information.

Orientation: Determine what the data means. Use a combination of analytical and intuitive responses to update your understanding of what's happening.

Decision: Determine what course of action you need to take to get the best result.

Action: Follow through on your decision.

The model is cyclical and requires managers to evaluate the outcome of the action and repeat the orientation, decision-making and action stages until the desired result is achieved. Boyd stresses the importance of not using the model in a static fashion but as a dynamic, fast, reactive model. He suggests that the faster pilots moved through the model, the more likely it is that they would get a positive result.

HOW TO USE IT

■ Unlike in air combat there is seldom the need for instantaneous decisions in business. Therefore, use Boyd's loop but leave the issue of speed to one side.

■ Start by identifying any opportunities or threats you face. You may already have an example on your desk or you could use a SWOT analysis to identify one *(see Theory 65)*. Gather as much data as you can about the issue but beware of the laws of diminishing returns.

■ Remember, no matter how accurate your data is it will always be incomplete and your brain will filter the information further *(see Theory 84)*.

■ Don't be afraid to use your intuition as you try to make sense of the situation. This isn't guesswork; intuition or tacit knowledge is something that develops as a result of past experiences and learning and resides deep in your subconscious until you need it *(see How to get the most out of this book)*.

■ Recognise that any decision you make is really only your best guess of what's right at a given moment. Keep refining your decision and subsequent actions by repeating the OODA loop until you are happy with the result.

■ Before you use the OODA loop on something significant test the theory in a safe environment.

QUESTIONS TO ASK

■ How difficult do I find it to make decisions? Do I take into account all the information available to me or are my decisions based on gut reaction?

■ Do I need to change how I make decisions?

LUFT AND INGRAM'S JOHARI WINDOWS

Use to appreciate how important self-discovery and shared discovery can be in increasing understanding and trust.

In the 1950s two psychologists, Joseph Luft and Harry Ingram, developed a model for soliciting and giving feedback. The model is a 2 x 2 grid which represents things that a person knows about themselves on one axis and things that others know about them on the other axis. By plotting the levels of self-knowledge and the knowledge held by others the person can develop a greater understanding of their personality and how they are perceived by others.

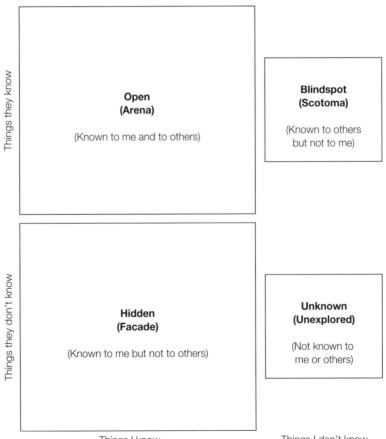

Things they know

**Open
(Arena)**

(Known to me and to others)

**Blindspot
(Scotoma)**

(Known to others
but not to me)

Things they don't know

**Hidden
(Facade)**

(Known to me but not to others)

**Unknown
(Unexplored)**

(Not known to
me or others)

Things I know   Things I don't know

Luft and Ingram designed a Characteristics Test that enables an individual to gauge the degree of things they know about themselves and to correlate this with the things their peers know about them. The responses can be mapped onto the grid to produce a window frame (usually with one predominant pane).

HOW TO USE IT

■ Use this model to analyse how good you are at giving and receiving feedback. Start by constructing your own window frame. Do this by accessing Luft and Ingram's Characteristics Test or any one of a number of online alternatives.

■ Examine the good, the bad and the ugly. The larger the arena pane, the higher the level of communication, understanding and trust between you and your team members.

■ If the arena pane is not the largest, then take action to increase the size of it by discussing your thoughts more openly with others and soliciting their feedback.

■ You also increase the size of the arena pane by reducing the size of the others. Remember you cannot consciously change what you don't know, so use self-discovery and shared discovery through giving and receiving feedback as a means of increasing openness, understanding and trust.

QUESTIONS TO ASK:

■ What's preventing me from sharing my thoughts with other members of my team?

■ How open are team members when talking to me about themselves?

THEORY 88   SMART GOALS

Use this simple tool to keep you and your staff on track and meet deadlines.

SMART is an acronym used to describe the setting of goals for individuals, teams or organisations. Whilst it is difficult to attribute the development of the tool to any individual, a number of sources refer to an article by George Doran in the November 1981 issue of *Management Review* as the first known use of the term.

Although there is no clear consensus on what each of the five letters stands for, the following are popular interpretations.

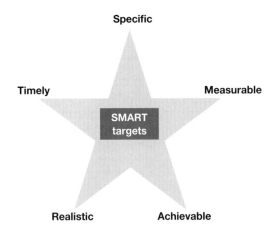

Specific: The goal is clear and unambiguous.

Measurable: There is a criterion that can be used to track progress.

Achievable: The goal is doable.

Realistic: The goal is relevant to the organisation and can be accomplished with the organisation's current resources.

Timely: There is a time frame for completion of the work.

The SMART acronym has been extended in recent years to include Exciting (making the goal challenging) and Rewarding (acknowledging everyone's contribution) thus making for SMARTER goal setting.

HOW TO USE IT

■ Firstly, make sure that every person has clear, well-defined targets. Woolly targets allow for ambiguity and misunderstanding. Get people to tell you what their targets are and correct any misunderstandings.

■ Once you are absolutely certain that everyone is clear on what is required devise a monitoring system that will track progress and identify when milestones have been achieved.

■ While you will want to stretch and challenge both yourself and the team, you must be certain that the outcome is attainable. Nothing demotivates more than constant failure.

■ Make sure that the targets you set for yourself and your team are aligned with organisational goals. If you don't do this you are unlikely to receive support from the powers on high.

■ Engender an appropriate sense of urgency by attaching a deadline for completion to each task/target within the milestone.

■ Recognise that the SMART approach to target setting is one of the simplest but most versatile tools you have in your toolbox; a bit like one of those multi-function knives that men buy as a luxury gadget and then find essential. You can use it for a multitude of activities including strategic planning, project management, setting team goals and performance reviews. Its great strength is that it gets you to focus on outcomes rather than activities/processes.

QUESTIONS TO ASK

■ How often am I going to measure progress against target?

■ What am I going to do if a milestone is not met?

THEORY 89   THE McNAMARA FALLACY

Use to remind you of the crucial role that non-quantifiable information plays in managing an organisation.

Robert McNamara was the United States Secretary of Defence from 1961 to 1968. He developed his fallacy theory as a way of explaining why America was defeated in the Vietnam War. His theory contains just four statements.

MANAGERS:
Measure what can be easily measured.
Disregard or poorly quantify what can't be easily measured.
Assume that what can't be measured isn't important.
Assume that what can't be measured doesn't exist.

McNamara believed that American generals and politicians had looked at the increasing number of Viet Cong killed and based on that believed they were winning the war. They ignored factors such as national resentment against an occupying army, a desire for independence and the high morale of the enemy; because such factors were non-quantifiable they were considered as of no importance.

HOW TO USE IT

■ Accept that since the advent of scientific management *(see Theory 3)* there has a tendency in organisations to base decisions on quantifiable information in the mistaken belief that such decisions are more scientific and therefore accurate than those that include non-quantifiable data.

■ When using statistics always ask how the data were collected and what assumptions were made when they were analysed.

■ Where relevant include non-quantifiable data such as staff and customer goodwill, reputation, staff morale and loyalty, knowledge and expertise of staff, the synergy generated by the unique mix of people who work for you (if any), value of internal and external personal contacts/relationships etc.

QUESTIONS TO ASK

■ What 'assets' does my organisation or team possess that are either difficult or impossible to quantify?

■ Do I take them into account when making decisions?

A FINAL WORD ON THE BEST OF THE REST

WHY PARETO WAS CROWNED KING

Managers are busy people. You are a busy person. Any theory that saves you time and helps you identify and access key information quickly has to have a value beyond rubies.

It's also a theory that can be used in a wide range of situations. For example: the 2012 Forbes Rich List of America reveals that the richest 400 people in America have a wealth equivalent to 12.5% of America's Gross Domestic Product. This means that about 0.000001% of the American population owns 12.5% of the wealth generated in America in one year. Based on that figure it's pretty certain that at least 80% of all wealth in the USA is owned by 20% of the population.

One thing you will always be short of as a manager is time so don't let other people's crises become your problem. You have your priorities and you should deal with them before you lend a hand to a colleague in need. Of course if it's your boss who is in trouble, his priorities are your priorities. Just make sure that he remembers your help.

Respect, trust and honesty should be the basis of your relationship with staff. Use feedback to and from staff as an opportunity to increase the level of openness and trust in your relationship with those you work with. However, if conflicts do arise don't leave them to fester and grow only to explode at the worst possible moment. Deal with them as they arise. How you communicate can either build trust and respect or inflame the situation further. The correct use of language, gesture and tone of voice is important in such situations. They carry as much meaning as what you say to your listener and provide your audience with an insight into your true feelings.

Use SMART targets with both yourself and your team to increase your chances of successfully completing any task and meeting deadlines. I've always admired IBM's old policy of target setting. Ninety-five per cent of each person's targets were fairly easy to achieve. This turned staff onto success and gave them the confidence to pursue the remaining 5% of targets which were much tougher to achieve. The psychology behind this approach seemed really insightful to me.

However, don't fall into the trap of believing that only financial targets are important. As Mark Twain claims Benjamin Disraeli said, 'There are lies, damn lies and statistics'. And often the most important information in a business cannot be reduced to figures on a spreadsheet.

Finally, while it's true that you learn more from your failures than your successes, you don't want a PhD in failure – no matter how much you learn along the way. Robert Townsend, who wrote the international bestseller *Up the Organisation*, reckoned that a good manager got 33% of their decisions right, 33% wrong and in the case of the remaining 34% it didn't matter what they decided as events would still have turned out pretty much the same. Now, he was the hugely successful Chairman and President of Avis Rent-A-Car but go on, admit it, you think you can do better than a one in three success rate, don't you? OK – go for it. If you don't try you'll never know how good you could have been.

THE ONE THEORY THAT SHALL RULE THEM ALL, AND WHY WE PICKED IT

AND NOW, LADIES AND GENTLEMEN, THE WINNER – THE ONE AND ONLY – TRUE EMPEROR OF ALL MANAGEMENT THEORIES IS: THE PARETO PRINCIPLE

Unfortunately Vilfredo Pareto cannot be with us to receive his award. Given his absence we feel that an explanation of our choice is required.

The one commodity that managers lack more than any other is time. Any theory that will save you time and help direct your efforts to where they will have the greatest impact has to be a winner.

The Pareto Principle separates the important few from the unimportant many. It shines a light on those few processes and people that cause you most of your problems. Sort out the 20% causing problems and watch your 'to-do' list shrink.

Pareto also identifies where to devote your energies in terms of developing positive factors. Use it to identify the 20% of products that generate 80% of your sales. This information can guide your decisions regarding the allocation of scarce resources. It can identify the 20% of your customers that generate 80% of your income. It is these people that you never want to upset. Pareto also helps you identify the 20% of your staff who are the real stars of your team and who should be recognised and rewarded.

The Pareto Principle is extremely elegant in its simplicity and has shown over the years that it can be applied to virtually any situation. A true all-rounder. Of course the split may not be exactly 80/20 but it will be in that ball park. Try it out on a range of issues and prove for yourself how all-pervasive the ratio appears to be.

A VERY FINAL WORD

Are you one of the 20% who have read the book in its entirety? Or are you one of the 80% who have read 20% of the book? Either way we hope you found something in it that you can use. But what does this book really tell you about management?

Writing it we identified seven key themes that seemed to keep coming up. These encapsulate what we think management is all about. They are:

1 Every manager must be true to their essential nature. Unfortunately it's not easy to uncover your essential nature. We play games with ourselves all the time and ascribe noble motives to despicable actions just so we can sleep well at night. The best managers know exactly who they are and what they stand for. To discover who you are will require some soul-searching.

2 Managers need to know their staff: what makes them tick; what their strengths and weaknesses are; what motivates them; what their interests are. If a manager doesn't know and understand their staff then they are operating blind!

3 Managers and staff must trust and respect each other. Trust and respect are not things that you can demand from people. Both of them have to be earned. As a manager the quickest way you can earn your staff's trust and respect is to demonstrate that you will not sacrifice any of them just to get out of a sticky situation or achieve your own personal objectives.

4 Managers and staff need a target to work towards. Some may call it a vision. I think of it as a purpose. A purpose gives people a reason, other than earning a living, to get up in the morning and go to work. It's what keeps them at work until everyone else has gone home – even though they aren't paid overtime.

5 People need to believe that their work has meaning and has been recognised. Too often the only feedback they get is a rollicking when they fail. Provide positive feedback whenever it has been earned and staff will grow and develop before your very eyes.

6 Achieving a personal objective is great, especially when it's something you have been working towards for years. But the downside is that no one can ever truly appreciate what you achieved because they

weren't part of it. That's why succeeding as a team is so much more satisfying. You can share your success with a group of people who truly understand and appreciate what you did because they were in the trenches with you.

7   Work is important but no one on their deathbed ever said 'I wish I'd spent more time in the office'. So keep work in perspective. It's important, but life is meant to be enjoyed. If you don't enjoy your work get out and find a job that contains both meaning and enjoyment – even if you have to take a pay cut. Life will be sweeter, I promise you, and you'll be a better manager for it.

FURTHER READING

Over the years we've found the following books both useful and a good read.

Berne, E. (2010) *Games People Play.* Penguin: London.

Cole, G. A. (2003) *Management Theory and Practice* (6th edn). Thomson: London.

Crosby, P. (1980) *Quality is Free.* Penguin: London.

Deming, E. (2000) *Out of Crisis.* MIT: Cambridge Mass.

Drucker, P. F. (2007) *The Essential Drucker.* Butterworth-Heinemann: Oxford.

Green, R. (2000) *The 48 Laws of Power.* Penguin: London.

Hayek, F. A. (2007) *The Road to Serfdom.* The University of Chicago Press: Chicago.

Handy, C. (1993) *Understanding Organisations.* Penguin: London.

McGregor, D. (2006) *The Human Side of Enterprise.* McGraw-Hill: New York.

Moss Kanter, R. (1989) *The Change Masters.* Unwin Hyman: London.

Northouse, P. G. (2010) *Leadership Theory and Practice* (5th edn). Sage: London.

Pugh, D. S. (2008) *Organisation Theory* (5th edn). Penguin: London.

Townsend, R. (1970) *Up the Organisation.* Coronet Books: London.

Van Assen, M., van den Berg, G. and Pietersma, P. (2009) *Key Management Models.* Pearson/FT Prentice Hall: London.

If you can't find one of the above texts in the bookshop or on Amazon try www.abebooks.co.uk

INDEX

achievement 64, 65, 79, 98
action-centred leadership 36–7
active listening 206
Adair, John 36
Adams, Stacy 68
affiliation 60, 64, 65
aims and ambitions 20, 21
Alderfer, Clayton 62–3
alliances 183, 185
Ansoff, Igor 152
assertiveness 224–5
assumptions 114, 115, 116, 197
Austin, Nancy 186
authority 4, 5, 24–5, 200–1, 214
   Monarchical cultures 112
   Urwick's principles 12
   Weber's tripartite classification of
      202–3
   see also power
autocratic management 88, 89
autonomy 67, 73, 78, 186

balance, between teams and
   departments 12
Baldridge, Malcolm 194
Balkanised cultures 120–1
Bandler, Richard 226
Barbarian cultures 112, 113
basic assumptions 114, 115
basic needs 60, 61
basic style theory 32–3
Bass, Bernard 50
Belbin, Meredith 84–5, 100
beliefs
   change management 133, 141
   charismatic leadership 46, 47
   expectancy theory 70
   group formation 92, 93
   OK Corral model 74
   organisational culture 104, 105, 114
   transformational leadership 48–9,
      50–1, 52

belonging 10, 11, 60, 61
benchmarking 67, 192–3, 197
benevolent-authoritative
   management 88
Bennis, Warren 52
Berne, Eric 63, 76, 78, 79
Black Country Quality Programme
   (BCQP) 196
Blake and Mouton's leadership grid
   34–5, 89
Blanchard, Ken 40, 54
blue sky thinking 138, 139
Boston Consulting Group (BCG)
   158–9, 174
bottom-up approaches to planning
   151
bouncing ball model 90–1
Boyd, John 230
Brailsford, David 148
budgets 148
Buffet, Warren 19
bureaucracy 18, 19, 93, 106, 109
Burke, Warner 140
Burns, James MacGregor 42, 48
business plans 148

cash cows 158, 159
chain of command 4, 5
challenge 98
change 28, 127–45
   cycle of 128–9
   eight-step process 136–7
   force field analysis 134–5
   incremental 190
   levels of 140–1
   organisational culture 122–3
   organisational metaphors 110
   Plan-Do-Check-Act model
      130–1
   scenario planning 172
   shadow-side theory 142–3, 144
   strategic management 156

change (*continued*)
  unfreeze-change-refreeze model
    132–3
  X and Y theory 16
change masters 129, 138–9, 144
Characteristics Test 233
charismatic authority 202, 203
charismatic leadership 46–7, 50, 51
charismatic power 204–5, 214
Charlton, Bobby 83
child/parent states 76–7
Churchill, Winston 137, 139
clarity 98
Clinton, Bill 31
club cultures 106, 107
coaching 36, 40
coalitions 136, 138
coercive power 204, 205, 214
coercive transactions 42, 43, 55
commitment 90, 91, 98, 168, 181
communication 15, 19, 88
  change management 127, 129
  impact on motivation 58–9
  Neuro Linguistic Programming
    227
  transactional analysis 76–7, 78
Company Men 86–7
competition 11, 121, 166, 167, 175
competitive advantage 164, 175
complaints 19, 185, 221, 223
compromise 224, 229
concern for staff 32–3
confidence 28–9, 30, 31, 205
  charismatic leadership 46, 47
  expectancy theory 70
  positive self-talk 79
  transactional analysis 76
conflict 94, 95, 96, 97, 101, 224–5,
  238
consistency 7, 17
constructive transactions 42, 43, 55
consultative management 88
contingency theory 38–9
continuity 12
continuous improvement 14, 190–1
control systems 117
co-operation 224–5
coordination 4, 12, 13

correspondence 12
costs 180, 184, 196–7, 221
country club management 34, 35
Covey, Stephen 20
Craftsmen 86–7
creativity 16, 61, 155, 169
Crosby, Phil 179, 184, 196
cultural beliefs 92
cultural web model 116–17
customers
  bargaining power of 166, 167
  Drucker's theory 14, 15, 174
  expectations 183, 197
  listening to 25, 187
  loyalty 175
  'multiplier' effect 180, 181
  Pareto principle 220, 221, 241
  Peters and Waterman's theory 18,
    19
  post-modernist approach 154
  staying close to 186

Dali, Salvador 219
Dansereau, F. 44
data, non-quantifiable 236–7
deadlines 33, 36, 85
Deal, Terrence 108
decision making 230–1, 239
delegating 40, 41, 222, 223
deletion 226, 227
Deming, William Edwards 130, 179,
  180–1, 196
demotivation 11, 22, 66, 69, 78, 235
direction 40–1
discipline 4, 5, 36, 190
discontent 68–9, 78–9
discretion 38, 39, 187
Disraeli, Benjamin 238
distortion 226, 227
division of labour 6, 7, 8
dogs 158, 159, 174
Doran, George 234
dress code 118, 119, 207
Drexler, Allan 90
Drucker, Peter 14–15, 24, 174

economic changes 170
efficiency 8, 9, 24

Egan, Gerard 142–3, 144, 163
ego states 76–7, 79
Einstein, Albert 24
Eisenhower, Dwight D. 58, 219,
    222–3
emotional intelligence 228–9
emotions 69, 74–5, 76, 127, 128
empathy 228, 229
England rugby team 101
environmental issues 170
equity 6, 7, 68–9
ERG theory 62–3
Ernst, Franklyn 74
espoused values 114, 115
esteem 60, 61
European Foundation for Quality
    Management (EFQM) 194, 195
Excellence Model (Baldridge) 194–5
Excellence Model (Peters, Waterman
    & Austin) 186–7
existence, relatedness and growth
    (ERG) theory 62–3
expectancy theory 70–1
expert knowledge 206, 207
expert power 204, 205
exploitive-autocratic management
    88, 89
external environment 100–1, 140,
    141, 170

fairness 7, 21
Fayol, Henri 4–5, 6
feedback 3, 65, 78, 108–9, 238
    critical 66
    FSNP model 94
    goal-setting theory 98, 99
    job characteristic model 72, 73
    Johari windows 233
    Neuro Linguistic Programming 227
    positive 61, 243
Fiedler, Fred 38
filters 226–7, 231
First Direct Bank 175
first impressions 207
fishbone model 131, 188–9, 193
five forces theory 166–7
5S housekeeping theory 190–1
force field analysis 134–5

Ford, Henry 8, 83
forecasts 172
Forming, Storming, Norming,
    Performing (FSNP) model 94–5
Forrester, Russ 90
French, John 204, 214

Gamesman theory 86–7
GB cycling team 148
generalisation 226, 227
goals
    Drexler/Sibbet team performance
        model 90
    Locke's goal-setting theory 98–9
    seven habits model 20, 21
    strategic planning 150, 151
    see also objectives; targets
Golden Rule 47
Goleman, Daniel 228–9
Graen, G. 44
Graves, Desmond 112–13
Grinder, John 226
Group Development Observation
    System (GDOS) 96–7
group development sequence model
    94–5, 100–1
group formation 92–3
group needs 36–7
growth needs 60, 61, 62–3

Hackman, Richard 72
Haga, W. 44
Hamel, Gary 156
Handy, Charles 83, 106–7, 122
Hargreaves, Andy 120
Hawthorne experiments 10–11
helicopter behaviour 30, 31
Hersey, Paul 40, 54
Herzberg, Frederick 66
hierarchy of needs 60–1, 63, 78
Hofstede, Geert 118
Homans, George 92
House, Robert 46, 47
human nature 16
Hurst, Geoff 83
hygiene factors 66–7, 78

IBM 238

idealised consideration 50, 51
idealised influence 50, 51
identity, sense of 83
Imai, Masaaki 190
implementation 90, 91, 153, 156
impoverished management 34, 35
individual needs 36–7, 106
inequity 68–9
influence 200–1, 206–9, 214–15
Ingram, Harry 232–3
initiative 6, 7, 13
innovation 18, 87, 187
inspirational motivation 50
instrumentality 70, 71
integrity 30, 31, 205
   charismatic leadership 46, 47
   reputation for 213
   transformational leadership 48, 55
intellectual stimulation 50, 51
intelligence 30, 31
interviews 207, 215
intuition 231
Ishikawa, Kaoru 131, 188, 193

Jensen, Mary 94
job characteristic model 72–3
job definitions 12
job rotation 73
job satisfaction 16
job security 6, 7
Johari windows 54, 232–3
Johnson, Gerry 116, 150, 162
Jungle Fighters 86–7
Juran, Joseph 182, 220

Kaizen 190–1
kaleidoscope thinking 138
Kennedy, Allan 108
Kilmann, Ralph 224–5
King, Martin Luther 205
KITAs (kicks in the ass) 66, 67
Kotter, John 136
Kübler-Ross, Elisabeth 128–9

leader member exchange (LMX)
   theory 44–5, 55
leadership 28–55
   action-centred 36–7

basic style theory 32–3
Blake and Mouton's leadership
   grid 34–5
charismatic 46–7, 50, 51
contingency theory 38–9
cultural 112–13
Gamesman theory 86
leader member exchange theory
   44–5, 55
Machiavelli's guide to survival 210
situational 40–1, 54
team development 96
trait theory 30–1
transactional 42–3, 48, 55, 209
transformational 18, 28, 48–53, 55
see also senior managers
learning 110
legal issues 170, 181
legal-rational authority 202, 203
legitimate power 204, 214
Lewin, Kurt 132, 134
Likert, Rensis 88
listening 21, 22, 23, 25, 144, 206,
   229
Litwin, George 140
Locke, Edwin 98
loose-tight approach to staff control
   18
loyalty 46, 86, 175, 237
   leader member exchange theory
   44, 45
   Machiavelli's guide survival 210
   Monarchical cultures 112, 113
Luft, Joseph 232–3

Maccoby, Michael 86–7
Machiavelli, Niccolò 210–11
management by walking about
   (MBWA) 11, 22–3, 49, 122,
   129, 191
management style 3, 32–5, 54
   Likert 88–9
   organisational culture 104
   7-S framework 160
   team development 96, 101
managers 3, 5, 181, 243
   change masters 138–9
   Peters and Waterman's theory 18

power and authority 24–5, 200, 203
psychopathic 212–13
seven habits model 20
X and Y theory 16–17
see also senior managers
market share 158–9
Maslow, Abraham 60, 63, 78
Maturity Grid 184–5, 196
Mayo, Elton 10
McClelland, David 64
McCormack, Mark 22
McGregor, Douglas 16
McKinsey 7S framework 160–1
McNamara fallacy 236–7
meaningfulness 72, 73, 78
meetings 41, 49, 91
mentoring 36
metaphors 110–11
Michigan leadership studies 32
middle-of-road management 34, 35, 156, 157
mission 141, 150
modernist approach 152–3
Monarchical cultures 112, 113
morale 23, 67, 131, 237
Morgan, Gareth 110
Moss Kanter, Rosabeth 138–9, 144
motivation 58–79, 219
   achievement and acquired needs 64–5
   Drucker's theory 14, 15
   emotional intelligence 228
   equity theory 68–9
   ERG theory 62–3
   expectancy theory 70–1
   Hawthorne experiments 10–11
   hierarchy of needs 60–1, 78
   individual needs 36
   influencing people 206, 209
   job characteristic model 72–3
   management by walking about 22
   motivating and hygiene factors 66–7
   motivational skills 30, 31
   OK Corral model 74–5
   transactional analysis 76–7, 78, 79
   transactional leadership 43

transformational leadership 48, 50, 51
X and Y theory 16, 17

Nanus, Burt 52
NASA 55
needs 36–7, 58, 106
   achievement and acquired 64–5
   customers 182
   ERG theory 62–3
   hierarchy of 60–1, 63, 78
Neuro Linguistic Programming (NLP) 63, 219, 226–7
new entrants 166
new modernist approach 156–7

objectives
   Drucker's theory 14, 15
   goal-setting theory 98
   leader member exchange theory 44
   strategic planning 150, 151
   teams 85, 96, 100
   Urwick's principles 12, 13
   see also goals; targets
Ohio leadership studies 32
OK Corral model 74–5
Oldham, Greg 72
OODA loop 230–1
operational management 140, 141
organisational culture 104–23
   Balkanised cultures 120–1
   change management 136
   cultural leadership 112–13
   cultural web model 116–17
   group formation 93
   Handy's model 106–7, 122
   Hofstede's dimensions 118–19
   metaphors 110–11
   Peters and Waterman's theory 18
   risk and feedback model 108–9
   three levels of 114–15
   transformational leadership 52, 53
organisational structure
   cultural web model 117
   Fayol's principles 4
   7-S framework 160
   simple 186, 187

organisational structure (*continued*)
Urwick's principles 13

parent/child states 76–7
Pareto principle 131, 182, 183, 219, 220–1, 238, 241
participative management 88, 89
Patton, George 58
performance 14, 15, 90–1, 180
person-oriented leaders 32, 34, 88
personal development 62, 63, 67, 92
PEST/PESTLE analysis 93, 135, 170–1, 175
Peters, Tom 18–19, 22, 154, 160, 183, 186
Pharonic cultures 112, 113
Philips, Julian 160
physical restraints 92, 93
Plan-Do-Check-Act (PDCA) model 130–1
planning 101, 148–9, 174, 182
benchmarking 193
modernist approach 152–3
new modernist approach 156–7
post-modernist approach 154–5
seven stages of 150–1
political factors 170
politics, organisational 110, 143
Porter, Michael 164, 166
positive thinking 75, 79
post-modernist approach 154–5
power 24–5, 55, 200–1, 206
Gamesman theory 86
Machiavelli's guide to survival 210
need for 64, 65
organisational culture 104, 106, 107, 117
positional 38, 39
sources of 204–5, 214
stakeholders 143, 163
see also authority
Prahalad, C. K. 156
praise 16, 61
Presidential cultures 112, 113
prices 167, 179
priorities 20, 238
problem solving 84, 86, 189
productivity 67, 92, 186, 187

Hawthorne experiments 10, 11
leader member exchange theory 44
scientific management 8, 9
profit 14, 180, 181
promises 70, 71, 79, 129
psychopaths 212–13, 215

quality 179–97
Baldridge's Excellence Model 194–5
benchmarking 192–3
fishbone model 188–9
Kaizen 190–1
Maturity Grid 184–5, 196
Peters et al's Excellence Model 186–7
quality trilogy 182–3
seven deadly diseases 180–1
question marks 158, 159
Quinn, James 156, 157

Raleigh, Sir Walter 25
Ramsey, Alf 83
Ratners 117
Raven, Bertram 204, 214
recognition 66, 67, 137, 138, 139, 150
regression 63, 79
relatedness 62
remuneration 6, 7, 66, 78
see also rewards
reporting 39, 117, 153
resources 5, 36
Drucker's theory 14, 15
group formation 92, 93
Pareto principle 241
team 85
Urwick's principles 13
respect 5, 10, 11, 21, 51, 187, 238, 243
responsibility
change masters 139
Drucker's theory 14
as leadership skill 30, 31
motivation and 67, 72
Urwick's principles 12, 13
X and Y theory 16

rewards
control systems 117
expectancy theory 70, 71
matched to effort and
achievement 79
power to grant 204, 205
strategic planning 150
transactional leadership 42
X and Y theory 16, 17
see also remuneration
risk 108–9, 131
rituals 112, 114, 116, 117
role modelling 46, 47, 91, 191
roles
role culture 106, 107
team roles 84–5, 100
Ronson, Jon 212
routines 116
rules 5, 16, 17, 95, 106, 107, 118,
119

scenario planning 155, 172–3
Schein, Edgar 114
Scholes, Kevan 116, 150, 162
scientific management 8–9, 237
self-actualisation 50, 60, 61, 62, 78
self-awareness 228, 229
self-belief 70, 74, 75
self-confidence see confidence
self-regulation 228
self-talk 75, 79
senior managers 25, 171, 196, 211
influencing 208
strategic management 152, 154,
156
support for change 137
see also leadership
seven deadly diseases 180–1
seven habits model 20–1
7-S framework 160–1
shadow-side theory 142–3, 144, 163
Shewhart, Walter 130
Sibbet, David 90
situational leadership 40–1, 54
skills 160, 161
SMART targets 99, 100, 109, 193,
234–5, 238
social skills 30, 31, 228

social trends 170
span of control 12, 13
specialisation 12, 13
staff management 140, 141
stakeholders 142–3, 144–5, 162–3,
196
stars 158, 159
stories 116, 117
strategic management 140, 141,
148–75
Boston Consulting Group matrix
158–9, 174
five forces theory 166–7
modernist approach 152–3
new modernist approach 156–7
PEST/PESTLE analysis 170–1
post-modernist approach 154–5
scenario planning 172–3
seven stages of planning 150–1
7-S framework 160–1
stakeholder mapping 162–3
SWOT analysis 168–9
value chain theory 164–5
strategy 160, 161
strengths and weaknesses 52, 53,
100, 161, 168–9, 175
sub-cultures 106–7, 120–1, 123
substitute products 166
suppliers 166, 167
support 40–1
surface manifestations 114, 115
SWOT analysis 93, 135, 168–9,
175, 231
symbols 116, 117
synergy 20, 21, 205, 214
systems 160, 161

tacit knowledge 231
targets 15, 33, 36, 67, 243
goal-setting theory 98
leader member exchange theory
44
SMART 99, 100, 109, 193,
234–5, 238
see also goals; objectives
task complexity 98, 99
task compliance management 34,
35

task cultures 106, 107
task design 72–3
task needs 36–7
task-oriented leaders 32, 34, 88
Taylor, Frederick 8, 9, 192
team management 34, 35
team spirit 6, 7, 61, 101, 121
teams 83–101, 183, 244
    change masters 138, 139
    cross-functional 186, 187
    Drexler/Sibbet team performance
        model 90–1
    Gamesman theory 86–7
    group development 94–5, 96–7,
        100–1
    group formation 92–3
    Locke's goal-setting theory 98–9
    organisational culture 106
    situational leadership 41
    synergy 20
    team management style 88–9
    team roles 84–5, 100
technology 24, 92, 164, 170
'thank-you', saying 41, 67
Thomas, Kenneth 224–5
time 238, 241
top-down approaches to planning
    151
Total Quality Management (TQM)
    180, 182, 197
Townsend, Robert 239
Toyota 173
traditional authority 202, 203, 214
training 8, 9, 36, 61, 129
trait theory 30–1
transactional analysis 76–7, 78, 79
transactional leadership 42–3, 48,
    55, 209
transformational leadership (TL) 18,
    28, 48–53, 55
Truman, Harry S. 201
trust 5, 31, 238, 243
    conflict resolution 225
    management by walking about 22

teams 90, 91
transformational leadership 48, 52,
    53, 55
Tuckman, Bruce 94, 100

uncertainty 154, 155, 157, 184
unfreeze-change-refreeze model
    132–3
unity of direction 4, 5
Urwick, Lyndall 12

valence 70, 71
value chain theory 164–5
values
    change management 133, 141
    charismatic leadership 46, 47
    group formation 92, 93
    impact on motivation 58
    organisational culture 104, 105,
        114, 115
    organisational metaphors 110
    Peters and Waterman's theory 18,
        19
    shared 161
    team development 96, 97
    transformational leadership 50, 51,
        52, 53
vision 52, 53, 55, 141, 243
    change masters 138, 139
    eight-step approach to change
        136, 137
    strategic planning 150
Vroom, Victor 70–1

Waterman, Robert 18–19, 154, 160,
    186
Weber, Max 47, 202–3
Wheelan, Susan 96, 100
win-win solutions 20, 21, 95, 209
Wittingham, Richard 162
Woodward, Clive 101
work rotation 73

X and Y theory 16–17